PERSUASION

PERSUASION

A NEW APPROACH TO CHANGING MINDS

ARLENE DICKINSON

Collins

Persuasion

Copyright © 2011 by 761250 Alberta Ltd.

All rights reserved.

Published by Collins, an imprint of HarperCollins Publishers Ltd.

First edition

The lyrics quoted on page vii are from "You've Got a Friend" by Carole King.

HarperCollins books may be purchased for educational, business, or sales promotional use through our Special Markets Department.

HarperCollins Publishers Ltd.
2 Bloor Street East, 20th Floor
Toronto, Ontario, Canada
M4W 1A8

www.harpercollins.ca

Library and Archives Canada Cataloguing in Publication

Dickinson, Arlene
Persuasion / Arlene Dickinson.

ISBN 978-1-44340-596-6

1. Dickinson, Arlene. 2. Persuasion (Psychology). 3. Success in business—Canada. 4. Businesswomen—Canada—Biography. I. Title.
HC112.5.D53A3 2011   338.092   C2011-903637-1

Printed and bound in the United States
RRD 9 8 7 6 5 4 3 2 1

To my children, Garrett, Michael, Carley and Marayna.
"Winter, Spring, Summer or Fall . . ."
With all the love in my heart.

Contents

PERSUASION

Introduction

How do you convince someone to do what you want, in a way that leaves both of you feeling good about it? I make a living trying to answer that question. My job as a marketer is to help companies and organizations establish and define their brands, then persuade the marketplace in general and consumers in particular to pay attention. So persuasion is something I understand, because when you get right down to it, it's really what marketing is all about.

But figuring out how to persuade others isn't just my day job. It's also how I pulled myself out of poverty armed with nothing more than a high school diploma.

My path to becoming a CEO and one of the venture capitalists on *Dragons' Den* was not exactly linear. It zigzagged, crazily sometimes, and I've stumbled many times. But at critical moments along the way, I've been able to convince key people to take a chance on me or stick by me. And that has made all the difference.

Before any of that, though, I had to persuade myself I belonged in the business world in the first place. Let's just say it was a hard sell. There was nothing in my background to suggest I had what it took to succeed in business, much less run a company. I grew up poor, was a mediocre student, and moved out on my own after graduating from high school at age 16. My father predicted, memorably, "You're going to be barefoot and pregnant the rest of your life because you don't have a university degree." At the time, I didn't care. Back then, my only goal in life was to find a husband and have children. And there I *did* succeed: by 19, I was married, and I had my first child a few weeks after my 21st birthday.

By the time I was 27, I had four kids and was stuck in yet another dead-end job. I wasn't a good employee, I have to admit. I've been fired more times than I care to remember. I was forever challenging conventional wisdom and coming up with my own way of doing things, which is great when you're an entrepreneur but not so great when you're earning minimum wage and really need the money to feed your family.

The only job I managed to hang on to for any length of time was so horrible, they couldn't find anyone else to do it: I was a bill collector. I worked out of my kitchen with my children—all under the age of six—roaring around in the background. I'll never forget sitting at my Formica table, staring at the fridge (avocado green, of course, and plastered with the kids' drawings and pictures), and steeling myself to dial someone's number. This was in the days when phones were attached to the wall, but I'd purchased an extra-long cord—princess pink, to match the phone—so when the kids blasted through the room, I could run around the corner to try to get away from the noise.

I'd received collection calls myself—we were perpetually broke—and frankly, I found it really difficult to make them. I felt too sorry for the people who'd overextended themselves and just didn't have the money. They were apologetic and embarrassed usually, and frustrated because they genuinely wanted to pay their bills but just weren't able to. I'd listen to their stories and wind up sympathizing instead of pressing them for cash. The rest of the people on my call list, the deadbeats, just made me angry. With them, it was pointless: they seemed to get pleasure from cursing at me and clearly had no intention of forking over a penny. But sometimes I even ended up feeling sorry for them, too. What had happened in their lives to make them that way?

The worst part of the job was when I had to pile everyone into my beat-up old car and drive out to someone's farm to serve a summons. Dogs would chase the car up the driveway, one of the kids always suddenly needed to go to the bathroom, and the people who answered the door usually looked either scary or simply so battered by misfortune that I felt like a terrible person for contributing to their despair. It was depressing, not least because I felt that I was staring down the barrel at the kind of life I was one step away from myself.

Frankly, I might be living a life like that today if I hadn't got divorced when I was 31. It turned out to be my catalyst for change. Here's why: a family court judge told me that before I could have my kids with me full time, I needed to prove I could support them—and I was absolutely determined to have my kids with me full time.

Every one of us has events in our lives that change who we are. Those events can become a negative or a positive influence, depending on whether we choose to use them as engines for propulsion or excuses for defeat. While it would have been easy to have a "woe is me" reaction to a failed marriage and an acrimonious custody battle, I decided to view my circumstances as a springboard: I had four amazing children who needed me, and I had to try, at the very least, to make enough money to take care of them. Everything I have done and built since has been because of my need to ensure my children were taken care of and loved.

This does not mean I've always been the best mother. Just ask my kids! They have lots of good stories about me falling short. I was a young mom, after all, and I fumbled and improvised a lot. But there was never any question that my children were my purpose in life. Getting married as a teenager and having four kids in short order created a lot of challenges. But it also drove me to transform my life.

In 1987, I lost everything in my life that had previously signified identity: my home, my husband, and my role as primary caregiver to my kids. The only jobs I'd ever had were clerical or administrative. I had no idea what else I could do. Or even wanted to do. I could not even have dreamed that, one year later, I'd be a partner at Venture Communications, then a tiny Calgary agency. But that's what happened. Ten years on, I became CEO, and today, Venture has grown to become one of the largest independent marketing firms in Canada.

How did I do it? I'll explain in detail in the chapters to come, but here's the short answer: I figured out how and why principled persuasion works. The most incredible thing about it, as far as I can tell, is how easy it is. You don't need to be brilliant or a dazzling wordsmith or drop-dead gorgeous. You don't have to be an extrovert or wildly charismatic. It doesn't require an MBA or a background of wealth and privilege. To be a good persuader all you need to be is self-aware, willing to be honest even when telling the truth is difficult, and committed to reciprocity in all your relationships.

In other words, just about anyone can do it. And it can help you in just about any situation you find yourself in, in business and the rest of life.

PERSUASION IS ALL ABOUT RELATIONSHIPS

Over the years in marketing, I've learned that customers are persuaded to reach for a particular brand in the store because it represents something larger to them: good health, or happiness, or sophistication, or whatever the case may be. People who gravitate toward a Nike running shoe, for instance, aren't focused on the quality of the rubber used to make the sole or the strength of the reinforcements around the shoelace holes. They're not attracted by specific features, but rather by the benefit the shoe promises: victory. Their connection to the brand is primarily emotional.

So as a marketer, I think about persuasion in terms of creating an emotional connection—a relationship—between a company and a consumer. And I tell clients that as with any relationship, if you want it to work, you'd better be true to your own values and honest with the other party, and you'd better make sure there's something in it for both of you.

Those same three conditions—authenticity, honesty, reciprocity—provide the bedrock of principled persuasion in everyday one-on-one business situations, too, whether you're trying to land a new client or convince your boss to give you a raise. But there are some pretty big differences between persuading 100,000 people to buy a certain brand of detergent and persuading a particular individual to give you work or loan you money or see things your way.

The first difference is chemistry, which is key to one-on-one persuasion. While market research isn't foolproof, it does allow you to craft a message that will (theoretically anyway) appeal to a broad range of people. In everyday situations, though, what's persuasive to one person may be a complete turnoff to another. On *Dragons' Den*, an entrepreneur sometimes comes on the show seeking backing for an idea that leaves me cold but whips one of the other four dragons into a frenzy. And vice versa. Our responses may have nothing to do with the financial viability of the idea and everything to do with the pitch itself—and our gut reactions to the entrepreneur. Sometimes, for reasons I may not be able to put my finger on but have learned over the years not to ignore, I just don't trust the pitcher.

The second difference between persuading markets and persuading individuals has to do with the number of variables you can control. Meetings with clients, job interviews, negotiations with neighbours—these aren't tightly scripted exercises featuring gorgeous celebrities, fluent voice-overs, and crisp visuals. They're dynamic human interactions where anything can happen. Maybe you've been up most of the night with a sick child and just aren't on your game. But if you flub a word or forget one of your main points, there's no do-over. Then there's the unpredictability of the person you're trying to persuade: perhaps he's one of those terminally bored types who won't make eye contact—or the type who fires off a volley of questions before you even have a chance to sit down. And for all you know, he's feeling snappish because *he* was up most of the night with a sick child. The other person's mood, temperament, and personality all affect the interaction, and you have to adapt accordingly.

Or to put it another way: everyday persuasion is intricate, complex, and requires improvisational skills. Yet you're already doing it all the time, maybe without even being aware of it. "Eat your broccoli, then you can have dessert." "Honey, I just read a great review of that new French restaurant—want to go there instead of the sports bar?" Trying to get the bank manager to extend a line of credit to carry you through a rough patch, asking your book club to read something a little lighter this time, convincing your kids to turn off the video game and go kick a soccer ball around—they all involve persuasion.

Although many people think of persuasion primarily as a business skill, and one that's required mostly by salespeople and lawyers, the truth is that it plays a huge role in everyone's everyday life and in virtually every line of work. Unless you live in complete isolation on a desert island, you have to interact with other people—co-workers, clients, bosses, customers—and many of those interactions involve persuasion. First off, you need to persuade someone to give you a job. And then you need to persuade a manager to let you keep it, or change it, or move up—not to mention the countless daily acts of persuasion at the office: getting a colleague to help on a project or to back off, convincing the boss to listen to your idea or overlook your mistake, asking the administrative assistant to stay late to help stuff envelopes so the mailing goes out on time.

So if we're all persuading others so much of the time, why aren't we better at it? Why are some people naturals, while others come off as self-serving and aggressive—or, conversely, so unassertive that no one pays attention? The main difference is that people who are persuasive understand they aren't selling an idea or demanding results or pleading to be heard. *They know they're building relationships founded on an emotional connection.* And there's always something in it for everyone.

Good persuaders recognize that it's not just about what they want but what they have to offer others. They understand that it's not only about self-interest—it's also about getting others to see that what you want is actually in their best interests, too. They help people figure out how to do things together with a shared sense of purpose. Like leaders, they inspire, but persuaders have a different goal: they seek collaboration, not domination.

Or to put it another way, persuaders want partners, not followers.

CONNECT
....

When Hugh Laurie, star of the TV show *House* (and one of my favourite actors), won a Golden Globe in 2007, he said that business "is not about whether or not you do good work. It's about whether or not you get the *chance* to do good work."

I agree. And I believe that creating an emotional connection is one of the best ways to convince someone to give you that chance—and build a partnership. When a potential client asks Venture to bid on a project, we know we're up against other firms that are also capable of delivering great work. There's a lot of talent out there. And we're all asking ourselves the same questions. What would give us the edge: Working longer hours? Outsourcing to keep costs down? Those things might help. Very often, though, the deciding factor will be a chemistry test: which firm or individual the client feels most comfortable with on a personal level. You're embarking on a relationship, after all. If you connect personally, your interactions are going to be more pleasant and the relationship could also wind up being a lot more productive and creative. So when I'm trying to convince someone to hire us, one thing I focus on is creating an emotional connection.

Now, when I talk about an emotional connection, I'm not talking about the type of relationship in which you reveal your innermost secrets in long, soul-baring conversations. I'm sure not suggesting you go into a business meeting and start confiding about the trouble you're having with your in-laws or your spouse's struggle to stop drinking or the cute thing your daughter said yesterday. Save all that for dinner with friends.

What I'm referring to is more along the lines of the kind of emotional connection you hope to have with your family doctor: it's not about intimacy but about feeling at ease. You don't need to know a thing about your doctor's personal life in order to feel a sense of connection and safety. We all know that it makes a really big difference if you feel comfortable with your doctor. While some MDs have a reputation for brilliance, the feeling you get in their examining rooms is that you're viewed as a case, not a person. They listen mechanically to your symptoms, make a quick diagnosis, and send you on your way. Somehow you forget to ask all your questions, or don't feel you can. The whole interaction feels perfunctory and rushed. Other physicians aren't eminent, but they take the time to listen and can explain things in terms you understand. They ask more questions, and you get the feeling they're really trying their hardest to figure out what's going on. You never feel too embarrassed to talk about something, and overall the experience is just a lot more comfortable. Clinically, the person may not have the credentials of an expert, but the quality of the care you receive more than makes up for that. When we have a choice, that's the kind of doctor most of us seek out.

Likewise in business—or in any aspect of life, really. Most people would just rather work with someone who puts them at ease. And it's quite possible to have that kind of connection without ever even mentioning your personal lives. For example, I have a client who is on one level completely unknown to me. I have no idea whether she's married or single or has kids even. Yet I'd go to war for her. She's collaborative, communicative, listens objectively, and, when she agrees with my ideas, is willing to champion them throughout her organization. When she disagrees, it doesn't feel personal. And she's not inflexible: she's principled but her mind is open, so she can be persuaded to change direction if a valid argument is presented.

So no, I don't know whether she's into astrology or what her living room looks like. But the bond we share is deep and true. It boils down to two things. First, I understand what she views as challenges in her job and what she's trying to achieve, and she knows I want to help her get there. And second, it feels safe to be vulnerable with her:

trying out ideas that aren't yet fully formed, for instance, or admitting to finding a business problem pretty daunting. I don't have to worry about whether she'll exploit that vulnerability.

When you think about your best working relationships, the ones that have been most meaningful or most successful or have taught you the most, there is almost always an underlying feeling of emotional connection that cannot be explained solely by professional respect or mutual self-interest. It goes beyond liking someone's manner or sharing the same beliefs. It's about understanding and feeling understood. It's about mutual trust and respect. That emotional connection is why some people can persuade us to go the extra mile for them and with them, while others can't.

And this is what you want to focus on trying to create with other people because it will change your prospects not only in business but in every area of your life.

SO HOW DO YOU DO IT?

Ironically, though social media allow us to rack up long lists of contacts, they make emotional connection more difficult. Email, texting, Twitter—they're fine for conveying factual content but not for connecting. The possibilities for misinterpretation are endless: a short message can be misread as dismissive, an attempt at humour can come off as cruelty, and so on. Communicating this way doesn't help you forge a closer bond. In fact, putting it in writing can be an excellent way to avoid direct contact.

Establishing rapport takes more effort, and it also requires the real-time complexity of give and take. It's not about broadcasting your viewpoint via keyboard—in fact, it's not really about you at all. It's about taking the time to figure out what's driving another person:

where he's trying to go, what he cares about, what he views as challenges, what he should worry about less. An emotional connection means that you understand someone on a level that goes beneath the surface. Everyone knows what this feels like with a friend; if you're lucky, you've also experienced it at work. You're engaged, sometimes finishing each other's sentences and building on each other's thoughts. It feels safe to share ideas and ask questions because you feel valued and respected. You're able to brainstorm freely, since you're not worried that if one of your ideas is bad, the other person will conclude that you're an idiot or will use it against you somehow. There's real trust there.

Some people think that to be good at persuasion you have to be an expert or have a big personality or be a smooth talker or know all the answers. But just the opposite is true: listening and picking up on subtext are at least as important to building emotional connections as anything you say. You don't have to be an extrovert with extraordinary people skills. I'm not talking about working the room at industry events and coming home with as many business cards as you can carry. I'm talking about really listening to, and trying to understand, one person at a time. When it comes to persuasion, an emotional connection is worth a hundred business cards from acquaintances who don't feel attached to you. Just think how valuable an emotional connection is in the context of office politics, where having an ally who can read you and who has your back makes a huge difference in terms of how you feel about going to work every day and also in terms of how well you're able to do your job.

So maybe you're a little shy. Maybe you feel you have trouble getting the room's attention. (Or maybe you're used to dominating the room, in which case you may have the most to learn about this topic.) None of that really matters because the main thing you have to be in order to create the kinds of emotional connections that will enable you to convince others to want to work with you is a really good listener. Listening is the key to connecting.

BUT ISN'T PERSUASION REALLY
ABOUT CONNING PEOPLE, NOT CONNECTING?

Somewhere along the line, persuasion—the word itself as well as the act—got a bad rap. You may think of it as something underhanded, even a little slimy. After all, don't politicians twist the facts to persuade you to vote for them? And didn't a TV commercial persuade your son that a wildly expensive new toy—the same one now gathering dust under his bed—would make life a carnival? (And didn't he make your life a living hell until he finally persuaded you to buy it?)

Well, yes, that is persuasion. But it's not the kind of persuasion I'm talking about. *I believe the methods you use are just as important as the outcome.* Principled persuasion doesn't involve tricks, coercion, or shading the truth. And the result is win-win: both sides benefit roughly equally, and accountability is built into the deal. To me, persuasion is the honest, shared pursuit of mutual self-interest.

Good persuaders don't try to ram ideas down your throat or fool you with half-truths. They don't have to. You're compelled to listen to them because it's clear they're not simply promoting their own interests. They're also thinking about yours. They're looking to create a relationship that works for both of you.

So, no, there's nothing sneaky or deceitful about persuasion. Not when it means being straight with the other party and true to yourself, and not when there's something in it for both of you. Whatever your circumstances and aspirations, it's a highly valuable business skill that can help you get where you want to go, without selling your soul. It's also a social skill that's useful in all kinds of situations where you need to persuade people to give you a chance, help you out, and see the world your way. Whether you run a business or work in one, you have to persuade others that you and your company provide value. And whether you're a stay-at-home parent or a neurosurgeon, a CEO or a volunteer, you need to know how to persuade others to help you complete tasks as well as build something new together.

Let me show you how. In the following pages I share my framework for thinking about principled persuasion, so that you develop a greater awareness of when and how you can get others to see and do things your way—and when you shouldn't even bother trying. I'll also lay out the process of persuasion, from the initial preparatory stages right through to sealing the deal and delivering, so that you know exactly what to do and how to do it effectively. But before you can convince anyone else of anything, you need to convince yourself that you're worth listening to—and for many people, including me, self-persuasion is the biggest challenge of all. So we'll look at how to become better at that, too, so you stop unintentionally sabotaging your progress both at work and in the rest of your life.

Ultimately, principled persuasion is all about relationships, whether with co-workers or managers, siblings or friends. Learning to approach these relationships differently won't just make you more convincing. It can literally change your life. It certainly did mine.

PART ONE

TRICKS AND TRAPS

Getting to yes is the goal of all persuasion, whether you're trying to get the last seat on a sold-out flight or trying to land your dream job. But how you get to yes matters. Ultimately, if you have to do something unethical to get your own way, it's just not worth it, and it may well come back to haunt you.

Remember how Tom Sawyer tricked his friends into whitewashing a fence for him? His aunt had sentenced him to spend a beautiful summer day doing a chore he detested, but he had a novel idea: pretend whitewashing was not only great fun but also required extraordinary talent. Not just anyone, he told his friends, could paint a fence. Soon enough, all the other boys were begging to try their hand at it—and paying him for the honour. Tom sat in the shade while they worked, having a grand old time, and "if he hadn't run out of whitewash, he would have bankrupted every boy in the village."

Was Tom Sawyer a brilliant persuader? Yes. But people usually figure out at some point that they've been tricked, and they tend to get pretty ticked off (as in fact Tom's friends did, in Mark Twain's novel). If you're a fictional character known and loved for your mischievous ways, you might be able to repair the harm to your reputation. But in the real world, it's almost impossible. If people feel you conned them once, they almost certainly won't give you another chance. And depending on how ripped off they feel and how angry they are, they may not be the only ones who shut you out. If they spread the word, it will travel fast. You can't predict the repercussions: the same person whose opinion seems irrelevant today may wind up controlling your fate down the road. What you do now can affect your life tomorrow in ways you can't even foresee.

The importance of viewing persuasion through a long-term lens is a theme I'm going to keep returning to, for one simple reason: your most important asset in the business world is your reputation, and how you persuade others can make or break you. If your methods involve deception or intimidation, if your tactics are high-pressure or pushy, you can cause irreparable, long-term harm to your career.

In the following pages I outline common tricks and coercive techniques you should not use—and should not fall for, either. You'll learn how to recognize and sidestep traps set by others. And we'll also look at how to develop an absolutely crucial business and life skill: saying no. The goal isn't simply to help you become a stronger and more effective persuader. It's to help you learn to recognize and protect yourself from the Tom Sawyers of the world, by learning to attend to and trust your instinctive reactions and responses, which are usually dead right.

CHAPTER ONE

What not to do—and what not to fall for

I understand why some people think of "persuasion" as a dirty word. It's because most of us have at one point or another been talked into something that sounded like a good idea at the time, only to discover later that we'd been tricked. So I want to look really closely at less-than-ethical methods, partly to make clear what not to do when you're persuading, but also to help you recognize what not to fall for when someone is pitching you. Part of developing your own sense of ethical certainty, which is important in every area of life but particularly in business, involves knowing how to avoid being swayed by those who don't share your principles.

Unfortunately, trickery rarely announces itself, which is why we fall for it. In fact, it may look and sound quite a bit like principled persuasion. But it usually *feels* different to the person being pitched, and that's why it's so important to pay close attention to your gut reaction, not just the other person's line of reasoning.

Self-awareness is crucial in every scenario involving persuasion, whether the vet is trying to convince you to agree to additional tests on your dog or whether your manager is trying to talk you into taking on new responsibilities. In order to figure out whether you're dealing with principled persuasion or something else, you need to focus less on how you're being perceived by the other party and more on your own perceptions and instinctive reactions.

When a pitch contains an element of coercion or deception, you will likely have an instinctive response even if you don't intellectually recognize what's going on. For instance, you might start feeling that it's not safe to speak up. Or you might start feeling guilty. Or you might just start feeling panicky with greed, or fearful in some way that's difficult to pinpoint. These are primal reactions you should not ignore. I think of them as tip-offs that I'm in danger of being ripped off.

Gut instincts are frequently very reliable guides in life and in business, and it's particularly important not to ignore them in the two situations where you're especially vulnerable to deceptive methods of persuasion: first, where the other person wields power—or is trying to wield power—over you, so you're more likely to go along simply because it's the path of least resistance; and second, where what's on offer sounds amazing, so you want to believe what you're being told.

FEELING INFERIOR

If you're reluctant to speak up or ask questions when someone is trying to persuade you of something, don't dismiss your reaction. Usually it's connected to feeling inferior in some respect. The other person seems to know so much more. Or has so much more training or better connections or a longer track record or a fancier title. The more you listen, the more you find yourself thinking, "This must be a good idea—after all, he's an expert and I'm not." You stop saying anything because you worry that what you have to say might not only be wrong but might sound foolish. You stop asking questions because you don't want to reveal your ignorance. As soon as this happens—and I've seen it happen even to strong leaders—you've given up the most important thing you have: your own voice. If it no longer feels safe to venture an opinion or ask for clarification, you need to figure out what's making you feel this way: your own insecurities or the other person? If it's the latter, and someone is actively trying to intimidate you, you are definitely *not* dealing with ethical, win-win persuasion.

"Trust me, I'm the expert"

Pay very close attention when you feel intimidated; it can be a tip-off that something is not right. Of course, sometimes you're just feeling a bit nervous or are thrown off by an unfamiliar situation—grand boardrooms, car dealerships, and hospitals can all have this effect if you're not used to them. Other times, though, someone may be purposely attempting to intimidate you in order to get you to agree to something. I don't mean overtly threatening you; this isn't *The Godfather*. Something obvious would actually be a whole lot easier to identify and resist. What I'm talking about is more subtle, and the line of patter usually goes something like this: "This is a highly complex field you don't have a hope of understanding. But don't worry your pretty little head about it; you don't have to understand. We're experts, we'll take care of it."

Now, when people tell you this, their expertise may well be legitimate. Quite possibly they do know a lot more than you do about this topic. But you should *always* feel free to ask questions. If you don't, take it as a clear indication that it would be a mistake to proceed. If you don't fully understand what you're signing on for and someone is insisting you don't even need to know, it's not principled persuasion. It's coercion.

Fortunately, when someone is trying to talk you into something by implying that you're hopelessly ignorant, there are often some dead giveaways: a lot of six-syllable words, confusing acronyms, and impressive-sounding mumbo-jumbo. My rule of thumb is this: If I can't understand what you're talking about, I can't trust you. Real expertise involves the ability to take a complex subject and distill it to the point where it's accessible to everyone (more on this in Chapter 10). So if the person you're talking to makes you feel stupid, question the conversation, not your intelligence.

People who are honestly trying to convince you of something, rather than lord it over you with their expertise, will be able to explain things in a way you can understand. I have a friend who's a quantum physicist, a truly brilliant guy who spends his days thinking about how the universe started. And he's able to boil his work down to the point where someone like me, whose formal education ended at the age of 16, can understand it. In everyday situations, too, anyone who's trying to persuade you should be able to explain the reasoning in layperson's terms. Contractors, mechanics, realtors, plumbers, bankers—if the person really is an expert, he'll be able to explain things in a way you can understand.

Here's the deal: ethical persuaders who are aiming for a win-win outcome *want* you to ask questions. And they want to hear what you think because they need to be sure everyone is on the same page regarding goals and outcomes. They want you to understand what they're proposing before you agree because they know if you don't, it will probably lead to trouble for everyone in the long run. And ethical persuaders are always thinking about the long run because they care more about their reputations than about any one deal.

They know a short-term win is meaningless if it leads to a big loss down the road.

"Listen to me, don't talk"

Another red flag is fast talking, so quick and clever that you can't actually keep up with or absorb what's being said, much less get a word in edgewise. There's no give and take, just dazzling verbal pyrotechnics. This can inspire awe, but don't conclude that just because someone is highly articulate, whatever she's proposing is a good idea for you. I've learned the hard way that when someone is rattling on a mile a minute, supremely confident and apparently quite pleased with the sound of her own voice—I'm not talking about nervous babbling, which sounds quite different—it may be a sign of superior intelligence. And it may also be a sign that someone is trying to pull a fast one.

"I can't explain further, it's a trade secret"

Another thing to be wary of: any process that isn't open and transparent, or where the expert is tucked behind a curtain like the wizard of Oz. Let me explain by harking back to the early dot.com days, when Venture was hired by a company seeking to rebrand itself. At the same time, the management team hired a naming company (yes, people do make a living just dreaming up names) to choose the new company name. "This guy is amazing, an expert, so busy—we're lucky to have him," the client raved. "He's from *New York*." Now, a lot of people are bedazzled by out-of-town experts, as though living where the lights are a little brighter automatically makes someone better at his job. But it's a ridiculous notion. Being from New York doesn't mean you're smart, just as being from Tuktoyaktuk doesn't mean you're stupid.

I asked when I could meet this incredible man, and the client said he really didn't have time to meet with the likes of me, concluding, "Don't worry, we'll let you know how the naming goes." Um, not a great idea, I responded. Venture needed to be part of the process since we had to create a brand based on whatever name was selected. "Oh dear," the client sighed. "The thing is, his process is proprietary. He won't *let* anyone else in the room."

As soon as I heard this, I knew something was up and so talked the client into slipping me some of the names the naming guy had proposed, "just so we can get a jump-start on the branding process." Well, none of the names made any sense whatsoever. So I continued to dig and discovered that the consultant *owned* every single domain name for the company names he was proposing through his highly secretive process. He was squatting on and then reselling domain names after expensive "consultations." Our client went ballistic and fired him, but this guy is still in business. He gains credibility by being elusive, shrouding his work in mystery, and aggressively proclaiming his expertise.

One big problem with not being let in on a decision-making process (or any other kind of process, for that matter) is that you may discover too late that something's gone amiss. And by then, you may not be able to do anything about it. Anyone who's lived through a home renovation knows exactly what I'm talking about. You should always be privy to the process and know what's going on when you have a stake in the outcome.

"You can afford this, right?"

It's amazing how easy it is not just in business but in other areas of life to leverage someone's pride and use it against him. One technique is to start off by flattering you with the assumption that of course this business deal/ticket to the charity ball/pair of shoes is well within your means. Many people then feel too embarrassed to say they can't afford it or just don't feel comfortable spending their money that way. A deceptive persuader knows this perfectly well so will drive the interaction forward very quickly to ensure that the conversation rapidly advances to the point where it would be downright humiliating to back out. Which is why, if you feel at all nervous about admitting that you don't have the money or just don't want to spend it, you need to force yourself to do so immediately. Don't wait. You don't have to give a long explanation, and certainly don't feel you need to apologize. Something simple like "It's just not in the cards for me at the moment" is plenty. If the person persists and tries to shame you into a deal, consider it proof positive that you've done the right thing.

"Of course I went to an Ivy League university— the hard part was choosing which offer to accept"

I always say that if people who want to work with you spend more time talking about their own credentials than about you and your business, there's something wrong. When people need to tell you how great they are, where they went to school, how many VIPs they know, ask yourself, Why are they telling me all this, instead of what they're going to do with and for me? And if they're insisting that their qualifications are so amazing that you should shut up and let them think and speak for you, then trust your gut and ask yourself why. Do you feel tongue-tied? If you're afraid to speak up, it's never a good sign.

If you're star-struck, you're likely thinking, as I have at various points earlier in my life, "Gee, I'm lucky this luminary is even willing to help me; I'd better do everything I can to stay on his good side." For instance, when I was going through my divorce, I handed my whole life over to a lawyer who'd been highly recommended by a friend. I really questioned some of his decisions and the way he was handling my custody case but said nothing—what right did I, a mere high school grad, have to question the judgment of a highly qualified professional? I didn't want to tick him off. So I let him substitute his judgment for mine, and the price I paid for my silence was that in the end I didn't get sole custody of my kids.

As a general rule, unless you've been charged with murder and your lawyer is advising you to keep your mouth shut, it's usually a bad idea to let someone else speak *for* you. Or act for you, unless you understand at all times exactly what's being done and why. I'm not saying you should never delegate responsibilities—delegation is necessary and positive. I'm cautioning against signing over control of an entire aspect of your life or business to someone else, and relinquishing all responsibility for it because you've been convinced—deceived, actually—that your lack of impressive qualifications makes it just too difficult for you to understand and manage.

"Check out my client list"

An astonishing number of smart people have been hoodwinked into believing that handling their own finances is beyond them, as though compound interest were rocket science. Think of Bernie Madoff: he counted among his clients some of the most accomplished people in the world. Some were motivated by greed, of course, as his returns on investment were so high (on paper, that is). But many were attracted by his stellar client roster. With followers like that, the thinking went, he *must* know what he's doing.

Madoff is a great reminder that even if someone has an important reputation, you need to be certain that you're being persuaded by what he's going to do with and for *you,* not by what he's done or claims to have done for others in the past. The fact that people you respect have bought into something can be a promising sign. But it's never an indicator that you can skip due diligence. In virtually every scandal involving the mismanagement of other people's affairs, there are a few common ingredients: clients didn't just sign over responsibility for some aspect of their lives, they also failed to educate themselves about what decisions were being taken and why; and they didn't insist on accountability. Very frequently, they did this because they were wowed by someone's terrific reputation.

Life is stressful, business is complex, we all want to outsource headaches—I get it. But don't forget to ask yourself, Am I seeing value, or am I just assuming there's value because of the company this person keeps? How do I feel while talking to this person? Am I comfortable enough to ask a dumb question—or do I feel that just about anything I say is dumb?

FEELING GUILTY

Have you ever agreed to do something primarily because you felt guilty, then almost instantly regretted it? Say, serving lunch at your kids' school, even though it just about kills you logistically, because you feel guilty that you're not a stay-at-home mom? Or spending countless hours fundraising and volunteering for a cause because you feel you ought to, since your life is relatively privileged? Or stepping aside to give a colleague a bigger role because you feel bad that the powers that be make such a fuss over you but ignore him?

A fairly subtle comment—"I have a job, too, but serving on the PTA really helps me stay connected to my kids' lives"—can be enough to guilt you into doing something. It's not that hard to play on another person's concerns that she's selfish, or not doing enough to help, and therefore should be more giving. (I'm using feminine pronouns here for a reason: women are both more likely to encounter persuasion via guilt and more likely to fall for it because, even if we aren't naturally givers, the social expectation is that we should be.) This can be a form of moral intimidation, one that makes you afraid to say no. Sometimes, of course, the end goal is honourable—it's all for a good cause—but the means are not. In which case, the main thing you'll get out of it may well simply be feeling bad. Maybe not only guilty but also resentful, and that resentment might come out in some form that winds up undermining any good you do.

Guilt isn't always a bad sign. Sometimes it's a prompt from your conscience to do the right thing. I'm not saying that you should never volunteer, for instance. I give a lot of time to charities I believe in—almost always, disadvantaged kids are involved—and I don't for a minute regret serving on boards or fundraising or donating money. But I *am* saying that if you find yourself on the verge of being talked into doing something because you feel guilty, pause for a moment and ask yourself, Am I being persuaded? Or manipulated? Is this something I really want to do? If the answer is no, that's what you should say, too.

"But you have so much . . ."

If you find yourself considering doing something as a way of apologizing to another person for having more than he does—pause. Pay close attention to your feelings of discomfort and guilt. When you actually *want* to help someone—out of the goodness of your heart, not because that someone is implying you owe it to him—you don't feel uncomfortable or embarrassed. You feel happy and grateful that you're in a position to help out.

The single biggest mistake I've made in my career involved elevating someone beyond his talents and abilities because he made me feel guilty about my success. He told me that, so far, I'd just been lucky in business; according to him, since I wasn't well versed in business theories, I was headed for a big fall. Fortunately, he could prevent that with his scientific management principles—and I owed it to him, someone who actually knew what he was doing, to let him try. The implication was that I didn't deserve success and he did, and the only way to make up for the cosmic unfairness of having surpassed him was to let him run with his ideas.

Let's just say it took a long time to undo the harm this caused to my business. Take it from me: if someone is trying to persuade you of something by insinuating that you have too much and therefore owe it to him, trust your instincts. Ethical persuasion doesn't involve a guilt trip.

"But you don't really need the money"

Friends, family members, and even acquaintances may think nothing of asking a lawyer to review a document as a favour, or requesting that an electrician take "a quick peek" at a problem, or expecting an accountant to offer free advice, or a hairdresser to trim bangs, gratis. The line of reasoning is usually the same: "This is easy for you and therefore shouldn't cost me—in fact, you owe it to me, according to the unwritten contract of our relationship."

The problem with doing these kinds of favours, of course, is that word gets around, and before you know it, you're spending your weekends toiling pro bono for people who could afford to pay you. However, it can be hard to say no—you don't want to seem selfish or haughty. But unless you enjoy feeling resentful and put-upon, you have to figure out a way. Maybe it's "I don't mix business and plea-sure" or "I've learned it's a mistake to work for friends; it can really put a strain on the friendship." If that feels impossible, maybe there's the possibility of a trade or barter (which often has the added benefit of reducing the other person's demands on your time, as she now has to repay you in kind). Or perhaps you can say, "My normal hourly rate is *x*, but for friends and family I charge *y*."

Requests for freebies also occur regularly in the business world. Sometimes clients ask for highly detailed proposals and plans on spec. Sometimes they dump extra work on top of whatever you've agreed to do, saying, "While you're at it, would you mind . . . ?" Quite frequently, I'm asked to serve on new companies' advisory boards for free, the idea being that they're trying to get off the ground and I'm already established, so I should be happy to donate my services. My answer is always the same: "If you believe I offer value, then I should be compensated for my time."

Whether you need the money or not isn't the issue. The real issue is that your work has value and should be valued. Remember, anyone who is trying to make you feel guilty that you won't work for free is not practising principled persuasion—there's no reciprocity, no win-win. So you shouldn't feel obligated, either.

FEELING GREEDY

Only when you have a substantial financial safety net, or the risk is minimal, can you afford to assess a pitch without thinking about profits. Sometimes on *Dragons' Den* I have so much faith in the entrepreneur and/or the idea that my attitude is, who cares if I make a lot of money with this idea or not? But this doesn't happen very often, since business isn't about altruism. It's about getting a return on your investment. So it's not surprising that when someone pitches you, your thoughts automatically turn to the bottom line: What's the upside? How much could I make if I said yes?

However, feeling happy about the prospect of a win-win is not at all the same as feeling overtaken by greed. To me, it's the difference between having a normal temperature and a fever: when you have a fever, you're just not thinking straight. Con men know this perfectly well, which is why they try to whip you into a frenzy of greed, so that you're less likely to assess their promises analytically and more likely to make impulsive decisions. Although a principled persuader may occasionally resort to hyperbole, she does want you to consider all aspects of the deal, and what she's trying to get you to buy into is always a deal that has an upside for both of you.

"I'm going to make you rich"

There are very few, if any, business opportunities where for almost no risk you can make a fortune. If someone is trying to persuade you otherwise, my advice is to sprint for the nearest exit. I'll never forget how huge Bre-X, another Calgary-based company, was in the mid-1990s. After the company announced it was sitting on a gold mine in Indonesia, the whole town went a little crazy. For a year or so there, it was almost impossible to set foot in a restaurant without bumping into someone crowing about all the Bre-X stock he owned and how rich he was on paper. And then it was revealed that the whole thing was actually a massive fraud: the samples of gold had been faked. After that, it was almost impossible to set foot in a bar in Calgary without bumping into someone crying into his beer about all the money he'd lost.

I have made some lucrative deals in my time, and some bad ones, too. But I have never made a deal where I got something for nothing or next to nothing, and I have never bought into something that went from zero to 100 overnight. If that's what someone is promising you, don't let greed run away with your common sense. Business principles are essentially the same today as they were a century ago: it takes effort and strong values to build a solid company, and it doesn't happen in a day.

When someone is trying to get you to sign on for a deal that sounds too good to be true, bear in mind that it almost certainly is, and you're almost certainly not dealing with principled persuasion.

"This is an exclusive offer for a select group of people"

Any form of persuasion that stresses exclusivity and the company you'll keep may make your heart beat a little faster. Private schools, members-only clubs, and high-end financial advisors all make similar claims, and sometimes there are measurable benefits in terms of networking or the value of services on offer. But sometimes this is simply a direct appeal to your pride and desire for status, and the benefits will be minimal. Remember to ask yourself what, exactly, the win looks like for you, and whether the implied promise is too good to be true. This will help you figure out if you're being propelled by greed for status or by a real opportunity.

FEELING SCARED OR PANICKY

If you feel afraid or like you're being backed into a corner, you're less likely to be dealing with persuasion than with high-pressure sales tactics. Persuaders are accountable for results and delivering a win-win; there's reciprocity. Salespeople are accountable for making a sale, period. That's a big difference.

Sometimes it's perfectly clear that someone is trying to strong-arm you: "If you don't buy this deadbolt, someone could break into your house in under 15 seconds. You heard about the home invasion a few blocks over, right?" Or, "Operators are standing by to take your call; you have only two more minutes to take advantage of this incredible deal."

But other times, it's not so clear-cut. So you'll need to be attuned to your feelings, and if they include feeling alarmed, it's often a give-away that you're being bullied, not persuaded. Sometimes someone will try to instill fear or panic, then imply that what's being proposed will get you out of danger. Think of those pharmaceutical ads that frame what used to be considered everyday problems as medical conditions: "At a party, are you afraid to start a conversation? Finally, there's help. Ask your doctor about x drug." Healthy people are being encouraged to view their own pretty normal responses as medical problems—serious ones that require pharmaceutical intervention.

Unfortunately, coercive techniques can be hard to recognize and resist if you're primarily focused on your rising sense of panic: "If you don't understand how to use social media to promote your product, you're toast. Facebook, Twitter—that's the only way you're going to attract the demographic you need, and frankly, you're coming to this game late. We're probably the only outfit that can get you up to speed, but the time to start was yesterday."

When someone scares the bejesus out of you, you might forget to ask questions or might ask the wrong ones. If the danger is made to seem imminent, you just want it to go away. Think of the way fear of weapons of mass destruction was used to persuade Americans to support the war against Iraq. People didn't ask the right questions, particularly about what the long-term geopolitical and economic consequences might be, because the threat seemed so dire and so immediate. As it turned out, of course, there were no weapons of mass destruction in Iraq.

In less dramatic fashion, fear is often used to persuade teenagers to buy everything from soap to jeans ("You'll be a social reject if you don't have this kind"). And some teens use it to pressure each other into everything from drinking to having sex ("OMG, if you don't sleep with him, he'll just find someone who will").

So if a line of persuasion is making you feel afraid or a little panicky, don't disregard the feeling. It may be a tip-off that someone is trying to scare you into agreement. Sometimes, of course, the danger is real. For instance, your company really might need to create a profile that leverages social media, and fast. Or you might really be suffering from a debilitating form of social anxiety that would respond to treatment.

But a principled persuader doesn't need to make the danger seem more threatening than it really is, and always takes the time to outline the benefits as well as the risks of whatever solution is being proposed. When you're convincing, as opposed to coercing, you want the other side to understand exactly what's on the line, and you know that inducing panic won't help.

HOW TO SAY NO

Most of us feel uncomfortable saying no when someone is trying to convince us of something. What if the other person gets angry? Or decides you're a bad, selfish person? What if saying no leads to being rejected? Sometimes we're so afraid of conflict that it just feels easier and safer to say yes, even though what we really want to say is no. Unfortunately, a fear of conflict can make you an easy mark. It's not very difficult to bamboozle someone who feels he doesn't have a right to say no or who fears that saying no will make others dislike him.

Whether a neighbour is asking you to cut down a tree that drops leaves into his pool or a co-worker is trying to get you to switch shifts, you need to believe you have a right to decline—and that belief stems from knowing you have an obligation to protect your own best interests. Part of giving yourself permission to say no is recognizing when someone is trying to manipulate you, as opposed to persuading you.

Sometimes the distinction isn't all that clear in the moment, which is why it's so important to pay attention to your feelings and reactions. If you're primarily focused on pleasing others and avoiding unpleasantness, you may ignore your instinctive responses that should cue you that you're dealing with deceptive, exploitative, or coercive methods of persuasion. And if you are, you should not feel bad for even a second about saying no to whatever is being proposed. Who cares if an unprincipled person gets mad and winds up disliking you? The way I see it, that's a badge of honour.

I didn't always feel this way. I am an ex-pleaser, now in recovery, and I still slip up once in a while. But I've learned that, in business, you can't get around "no." You have to feel comfortable saying it, and the more successful you are, the more times you will have to say it. I think it's particularly difficult for entrepreneurs because it feels so definitive; there's always the worry that you're shutting the door that would lead you to the promised land. But resisting less-than-principled persuasion, even when it's really tempting, does have an upside. Learning how to say no in my professional life has made me much better at saying it in my personal life. It's no longer possible, for instance, to guilt me into attending an event I have no interest in.

This isn't to say that I have come to enjoy saying no. I still occasionally feel squeamish about raining on someone's parade, despite that during my time on *Dragons' Den* I've had to do so well over a thousand times. But one thing I've learned is not to drag my feet or try to soften the blow even if I feel uncomfortable. It's less distressing for the other person and less stressful for you if you get to no quickly and express it unequivocally.

It can be helpful to give a brief explanation of your reasoning, particularly if you want any kind of ongoing relationship with the other person. However, you can keep it pretty general—don't over-explain—and you certainly don't need to be blunt or hurtful. Unlike some of the other dragons, I think it's preferable to say, "I just don't think I can make my money back on this deal" than, "Are you on drugs? No one is going to pay $32.95 for a book of crossword puzzles about the music scene in the 1980s." You can be honest without insulting the person you're turning down. In any event, the more details you provide, the more likely people are to believe you are (a) inviting them to debate the merits of whatever they're proposing and (b) still open to being persuaded.

The key is to say no in a way that shows the other person you've heard and really considered the proposition but feel it just isn't a good fit. And always keep in mind that it's your right to say no if you haven't been persuaded of the benefits. You don't need to apologize for your decision and, in fact, agonizing and expressing remorse can make it more difficult for the other person to accept.

CHANGING A YES TO A NO

Occasionally in life you're going to have to reverse yourself and change a yes to a no. You agree to participate in a wedding or volunteer for a cause because someone puts you on the spot, then you decide that you just can't bear it and have to devise a way to get out of it. This happens in business, too, more often than people think. For instance, on *Dragons' Den,* it's sometimes the case that we agree to a deal on-air, but afterward, during due diligence, the deal falls apart. Things come to light that weren't disclosed by the entrepreneur—massive debts, say, or outstanding lawsuits. Or, upon closer inspection, her business looks really different from the way she represented it. In these cases, there's no choice but to reverse our decision to green-light a project.

It's never pleasant. Another person's anger or disappointment, however, is not a good reason to go ahead with something that just isn't going to work for you. But you should be prepared that the other person's response may be to try to guilt or intimidate you back to yes. For this reason, there shouldn't be a long preamble or detailed explanation of why you've changed your mind, and you need to be absolutely unequivocal. The more reluctant you seem and the more details you provide, the more ammunition you are providing to the other party and the more protracted the conflict will become.

For instance, I recently had to reverse a deal I'd agreed to on-air, after some facts came to light that made it crystal clear that it wasn't going to be a mutual success. I had to make a difficult phone call to the entrepreneur, who was, understandably, unhappy and responded with what seemed to me like veiled threats. "I don't want to have to tell people that you're not the nice person you seem to be on TV," is one that sticks in my mind. I had a thought then that was really helpful in terms of helping me keep my response unemotional yet also unequivocal: What if this phone call is being taped—would I be embarrassed if others listened to my side of it? Or would I come across as standing my ground calmly and courteously, in a principled fashion? I used that thought as my guide for the rest of the call, and it helped me focus on resisting intimidating tactics and staying the course.

OKAY THEN, WHAT FEELINGS ARE GIVEAWAYS THAT YOU'RE DEALING WITH WIN-WIN PERSUASION?

You should feel that you're dealing with a genuine person who's being completely honest and transparent with you. You should feel safe to ask questions and offer your opinion. You should feel that you trust him. You should feel, in other words, exactly the way you want other people to feel when you are trying to persuade them of something.

PART TWO

PRINCIPLED PERSUASION

Persuasion is an excellent test of character. What you will do and say, how far you'll go to convince others, reveals a lot about the strength and reliability of your moral compass. I have seen otherwise sane and ethical people throw caution to the wind and promise the earth and then some when they're pitching. I have also seen sane and ethical people turn their backs on highly lucrative deals for reasons that made sense only later. I believe a strong moral compass is the *sine qua non* of doing business, and without one, you don't have much hope of becoming more persuasive.

So explaining how to convince others to see and do things your way has to start with an examination of the moral framework that supports principled persuasion. Good persuaders are authentic, they're honest, and they're seeking a win-win outcome that benefits them and the other party equally.

Okay, okay, you may be thinking, hurry up and bring on the foolproof formula for persuasion! First, the bad news: there isn't one. Now the good news: this isn't one of those business books that relies on dry case studies and spells out lofty theories. Personally, I can't stand reading them—and certainly didn't want to write one. I don't believe any set of quasi-scientific principles actually helps you navigate the business world. There are just too many variables and unpredictable human dynamics in every situation. So I'm pretty skeptical of business blueprints with precise, sequential steps. And I've found that common sense and experience are better guides than ivory tower theories (in fact, the one time I let someone apply such theories to my company, the results were awful). So even if I had one, I wouldn't want to unfurl a blueprint for persuasion. There's just no way it could cover every situation.

Sales manuals often do spell out persuasion formulas, backed up by voluminous social science research that suggests we are more apt to be persuaded by two kinds of people: those who seem similar to ourselves and those who pay us compliments. Apparently, there are all kinds of little tricks you can use to get someone to think you're on the same wavelength, whether you are or not. One is called mirroring—when the other person crosses her legs, you do the same, and so on. The idea is to make your body language match, which supposedly establishes a feeling of similarity and harmony. Another trick is a classic sales technique. Try to find something superficial in common with the other person, then milk it for all it's worth to emphasize your similarity. This is why salespeople often ask if you have kids, or a dog, and then yelp, "So do I!" as though it's a remarkable coincidence. They also frequently remark on your good taste: "Cool earrings, where did you get them?"

I think these gimmicks are painfully obvious (not to mention difficult: ever tried purposely mirroring someone's body language? You'll feel like you're guest starring in an episode of *I Love Lucy*). When I'm trying on a dress and a saleswoman starts gushing about how good it looks, I don't find it persuasive. She doesn't know me, doesn't know what I normally wear or actually need, and doesn't care how I'll feel when I see the dress hanging in my closet, price tag still attached, a year later. Whenever someone lays on the flattery, my guard goes up.

The truth is, it's not really possible to devise a formula or even a set of tricks that will work every time because each time you persuade someone, the situation is different. It's an interaction, after all, so how you go about it will depend on the personalities involved, the seriousness of the matter at hand, and the nature and length of your relationship with the person you're trying to persuade. Obviously, your approach with a lifelong friend would differ quite a bit from the way you'd try to persuade an authority figure you'd never laid eyes on before. The variables are endless.

However, all principled persuasion does have three identifiable elements—honesty, authenticity, and reciprocity—and the process of persuading others can be broken down into distinct but overlapping stages. A note about wording: throughout the book I refer to the "pitch," by which I simply mean *any* occasion when you're presenting an idea that matters to you and are trying to get someone on board. Usually, I'm talking specifically about business situations, such as pitching for a job or pitching to land a new account, but a lot of my advice can be applied outside the boardroom, too, in everyday situations: talking to your next-door neighbours about their dog's incessant barking, say, or convincing your elderly parents to move to a retirement home.

And there's more good news, if you're the kind of person whose eyelids droop when you encounter one monotonous example after another. I'm going to explain what I know through my own experiences, which are not tidy, perfect illustrations of business principles where everyone wears pinstripes and speaks like a robot. My stories intersect, sometimes pretty messily, with real life, complete with mistakes and unintended consequences.

And that's one of my points: Your real life doesn't stop when you walk in your office door. You're still the same person you were when you left your house. As I've discovered, the lessons you learn in your private life can be instructive in the workplace. And vice versa.

This is something my dad, a teacher who valued knowledge above all else, taught me. He believed that learning isn't something that happens only in a classroom, in isolation from real life. In fact, when I was growing up, my father used to stop whatever was going on and point out the lessons to be learned, which he called "commercials." He'd say to my two older sisters and me, "Okay, time for a commercial" and highlight the teachable moment.

I remember walking home from high school one day and seeing fire trucks on our street. Our house was across the street from an elementary school, so at first I thought probably there was a safety demonstration going on there. But as I got closer, I could see grey clouds of smoke, and I realized the trucks were right outside our house. I started walking faster, then running. When I got home, out of breath, firefighters were pulling their hoses out of our house, which was still smouldering—and there on the grass sat my dad, surrounded by a bunch of little kids from the school. He was calmly giving them a "commercial" on fire prevention. My sister had been cooking with oil, not paying attention, when the cabinets caught fire and then so did the rest of the house. My father was the kind of person who'd take the time, even in the middle of a fire, to help you find the lesson instead of freaking out at my sister or frantically calling the insurance company or tearing his hair out. And he wasn't lecturing, it was just: "This is an opportunity for us to learn. Never wander off when the stove is on or you may wind up burning down the house." I'm pretty sure none of those kids ever forgot that particular lesson because it was based on real-life experience, not abstract theory.

What follows is also based on real-life experience—mine, complete with my dad's version of commercials. Here's the first: Persuasion is not about smoke and mirrors. It's all about authenticity and honesty, the building blocks of character.

Sounds simple, right? Well, not exactly.

CHAPTER TWO

Authenticity

J ust be yourself. It's what my parents told me when I was growing up, and likely what your parents told you, too. But as a teenager I couldn't figure out what the advice meant. I wasn't sure who I was yet, so how could I be myself?

To be yourself, you have to know what really matters to you and what you want. That calls for a degree of self-awareness that's rare at age 15—and frankly, not all that common at 25, 35, or even 45, for that matter. Some people spend their whole lives trying to be what others want them to be, or trying to be the same as everyone else. And they might be the nicest and most agreeable people in the world, but they are rarely the most persuasive. It's hard to believe in people who don't seem entirely sure who they are.

Good persuaders tend to be people who know exactly who they are and who, consequently, radiate authenticity. They're straight shooters who say what they think and do what they say they will. They're certain of their own principles and prepared to defend them.

You don't feel they'd ever try to deceive you, so the possibility of an emotional connection is there from the outset. Even if you don't agree with the specifics of whatever they're proposing, you're likely to give them a fair hearing.

Being yourself doesn't mean being sweet and nice, by the way. It just means not hiding who you really are. For instance, Kevin O'Leary, the most in-your-face dragon in the den, is completely authentic. What you see is what you get, which is why I can easily do business with him, though our styles are completely different and we frequently disagree. To put it mildly. He has no hidden agenda or motives, so there are no surprises. I think of it this way: Imagine you're taking a walk in the prairies through tall grass and a snake slithers out in front of you. You're not surprised—hey, it's tall grass, it's the prairies, there are going to be snakes. But if Ronald McDonald were to pop out suddenly, it would scare the hell out of you because you wouldn't be expecting it.

I'd far rather deal with an authentic snake than a wolf in sheep's clothing who's pretending to be all folksy and full of heart. There are a lot of wolf-in-sheep's-clothing types out there, and they're dangerous because they can lull you into a false sense of security, then move in for the kill. It's much better to know exactly who you're dealing with and what you're getting into.

In this chapter, we'll look at the link between authenticity and persuasion. And I'll do my best to convince you that embracing who you are, rather than trying to fit into a predetermined mould, can help you create the kinds of connections that will translate into greater success in business and the rest of life.

YOU DON'T HAVE TO BE PERFECT— AND NO ONE RELATES TO PERFECTION, ANYWAY

It's not uncommon these days to hear people talk about their "personal brands," but sometimes I'm not sure they really know what a brand is. Certainly a lot of business people don't. In fact, according to a recent Ipsos Reid survey of 1,200 business owners, more than half thought "branding" referred to a company's name or product, about a quarter said it means a logo, and the rest thought it referred to corporate image. But as I often tell senior executives, "A brand is just your company, seen through the eyes of others." It's shorthand for the way other people view a company, and you want to be sure the brand is consistent in every interaction, whether the interaction involves speaking to a receptionist or going on the website or buying a product. It's basically just the overall impression people have of a particular company.

For an individual, then, your personal brand is your essence, as perceived by others. Contrary to popular opinion, it's not something you can manufacture out of thin air. It's what others see, not necessarily what you intend them to see. Just think of the guy at the table who's trying to sell himself as the life of the party but is in fact viewed as an obnoxious loudmouth. Or the woman who views herself as elusive and mysterious but is perceived to be aloof and a snob. You want to be sure that what you're putting out there, and what others are seeing, are one and the same. There's a simple way to do this, of course: be yourself, and that starts with knowing and accepting who you really are.

A lot of people, however, are afraid to show who they really are, especially in a business situation—afraid that who they really are isn't quite good enough, afraid that revealing themselves will make them vulnerable. I couldn't disagree more. Authenticity inspires respect

47

because it takes courage to own who you really are, wrinkles, fat, insecurities, doubt, stress, and all. Being willing to expose your frailties and flaws along with your strengths, instead of trying to hide behind bluster or some other type of disguise, is generally a sign of confidence. You immediately establish that you're comfortable in your own skin, and your authenticity makes it easier for others to feel connected to you. They don't have to wonder whether you're faking it or trying to trick them. Being unafraid to be—and show—the real you is an act of bravery, and it's also pretty liberating. You're freeing yourself from worrying that others will find out all the bad stuff you've been trying to hide and deny.

So there's power in accepting your imperfections. It increases your ability to connect, for one thing. If you're concentrating on concealing something you find unacceptable about yourself, it's hard to focus on drawing people in. Actually, you don't want them to get too close—they might really *see* you. But if you're okay with yourself, and okay with people really seeing you—whether they like what they see or not—it invites respect. When people are willing to reveal themselves, they get my attention and I'm much more likely to listen to their viewpoint. Their ability to persuade me increases because it's clear there's no hidden agenda.

Here's the thing: the social science research I mentioned earlier is correct in one respect. People *are* more likely to be persuaded by someone they identify with. And most people don't identify with perfection. They relate to someone they perceive to be authentic, whether that person is similar to them or not. Even if others can't relate at all to your life and work experiences, they can certainly identify with and appreciate the fact that you're open, honest, and trying to connect in a real way. When authenticity is the hallmark of your personal brand, you're in the best possible position to make the kinds of emotional connections that underpin persuasion.

Embracing who you really are will take you further, faster, than trying to be the person you think others want to see. That's been my experience, anyway. It was only when I stopped trying to fit a cookie-cutter mould and trying to live up to the image of what I thought a CEO should be that my business really took off. Most of us tend to think of the ways we differ from the norm as liabilities, but sometimes they can turn out to be our most significant advantages. Over the years I've come to realize that there's another way to think about our vulnerabilities: not as weaknesses but as points of entry that invite emotional connections, and therefore as potential sources of power.

YES, I DO RECOGNIZE THAT FEELING VULNERABLE IS SCARY!

For years I tried to disguise and conceal my deficiencies, and lived in fear of being found out. I remember the first time Venture's head of PR came to me and said I needed to put myself out there a little more and raise my personal profile in order to raise the company's public profile. I froze. I didn't want to put myself "out there." I am by nature a private person, and was perfectly happy to be the behind-the-scenes force pushing the team to succeed. Besides, I argued, who would possibly be interested in knowing more about me? It just seemed the height of vanity—and potentially harmful to me as well as to Venture.

Talking honestly about my career would require revealing personal vulnerabilities, and the business world is, as you may have heard, a cut-throat place. Women, in particular, have to be careful to project an image of strength, to counter the stereotype of weakness and emotionality. I didn't want to risk my hard-won credibility.

I mean, what if someone discovered that I didn't have an MBA or even a university degree? What if someone took pictures of me and didn't Photoshop out all my faults? What if people heard about my failed marriages? (Yes, that was plural.)

How could I persuade the world to take me seriously if people found out who I really was? I had a picture in my head of what a CEO was supposed to look like, and I knew she wasn't supposed to look like me.

So for a while, when I gave speeches or interviews, the focus was always some aspect of marketing. I got pretty good at that, and expert at deflecting personal questions. But then a few years ago, I stood up to give a speech to a group of young women. I was planning to give my usual spiel, but when I looked out at this sea of expectant faces I had a weird sense of déjà vu. I remembered exactly what it felt like to be new to the business world and seeking guidance that could help me find my footing, only to receive a handful of majestic-sounding platitudes and a set of operating instructions I had no clue how to implement. I remembered that that made me feel even more inadequate, like I wasn't talented enough or smart enough to understand success, much less deserve it.

So with no idea exactly where I was headed, I abandoned my notes and went off-script. Way off-script. I said, "I'd like to talk to you very personally today. This is not something I'm comfortable with, but rather something I feel I need to do." I wanted to persuade them that a lot of their ideas about success were probably wrong, that they probably thought there were more barriers than there actually were. That most of those barriers were likely internal rather than external, and connected to subjective feelings of inferiority rather than objective gauges of relative merit.

So I talked to them in a real and honest way about how I got where I did, the odds I overcame, and the mistakes I made. I told them about being a single mom with four kids, the panicky despair of wondering how you're going to feed them, never mind put them through university. About struggling to find my way in the business world. About overreaching and expanding too quickly, then crawling off to the bank to beg for funding to fix my mistakes. About learning to be tough without sacrificing compassion, so that I could compete with the big guns in my industry.

The response I got to that rambling, off-the-cuff speech was unlike any I'd ever had before. I connected with the audience in a much deeper and more meaningful way, solely on the grounds of authenticity. I wasn't some business god, preaching from on high. I presented myself as I really am, someone whose path to success has not been smooth but who has persevered (and enjoyed the ride, most of the time). Since that day, I've learned there can be power—and freedom—in being willing to show who you really are. What I thought might discredit me has actually wound up *helping* me in business and also every other area of my life. People can relate to my story precisely because my history is not what you might expect of a CEO.

THE UNVARNISHED (AND UNPROMISING) BEGINNINGS OF AN ACCIDENTAL CEO

I was not born with a silver spoon in my mouth, nor did I have powerful mentors. I didn't even start out with career ambitions. This makes me different from many other CEOs, most of whom are, from a very young age, hungry to succeed in business. I got a career relatively late in life, for completely different reasons—as a means to achieve another goal, rather than as a goal in itself. I think of myself less as self-made than as remade.

But let me start at the beginning. I was born in Germiston, South Africa, a little town right outside Johannesburg. I don't remember much about it, beyond a vague, pleasant memory of playing outside and eating a lot of squash and avocadoes, which are still comfort food for me.

When I was almost three years old, my parents decided to emigrate. My father was an electrician, my mother was a secretary, and fortunately for me and my two older sisters, they understood the challenges of raising children in an incredibly complex and difficult social structure. They wanted something better for themselves, and for us.

We left South Africa and arrived in Calgary with about $50 to our names. My dad got a job at the phone company, we rented a home and lived in not-so-genteel poverty. Even when my father landed a better job, teaching electronics at the Southern Alberta Institute of Technology, he walked to work to save the 15-cent bus fare.

When I was five years old, I scored well on an aptitude test and my parents were advised that I should skip kindergarten; later, I was in an accelerated class that completed two grades in one year. Consequently, I was always the youngest and smallest kid in the class, which wasn't great for my self-image.

I was shy and very quiet and, as the years went by, acutely aware of how little we had relative to my classmates' families. My mom had a job, but she also had to make everything for us, from clothes to jam to bread. I remember whining, "Why do we have to eat home-made soup? All the other kids have Campbell's." (Now, of course, I wish somebody would make me homemade soup.) Groceries were a big deal in our home; sometimes we'd go two weeks without buying food. I wore my sisters' hand-me-downs and didn't own a new dress until I was a teenager. My sister made my prom dress, and it probably looked like it was made out of curtains, like something from *The Sound of Music.* But she and I both thought it was beautiful: white, with little purple flowers. (It's funny, now that I can buy all the clothes I want, that prom dress is still the item of clothing I think about the most.) When I recall the bright spots growing up, I mostly remember going to church together as a family and then having Sunday dinner. Although we didn't always attend church regularly, we were Mormons, and I loved the sense of being part of a community.

Often people who've grown up poor reminisce about how love compensated for a lack of material things. But there was always tension between my parents, and the climate in our house was sometimes chilly and silent, sometimes hot with anger. I think when you grow up in an emotionally chaotic environment, you're programmed from an early age to be attuned to others' feelings and needs. I tried to be invisible—the more invisible, the better, because it meant I wasn't causing trouble that could lead to an eruption. One good thing about watching from the sidelines, without the demands of playing a role, is that your intuition develops. You can sense when another person looks fine on the outside but is in turmoil on the inside. You can feel how the air changes when an emotional explosion is coming. (If only I'd known that growing up in a dysfunctional family was helping me develop the observational skills I'd need in the business world!)

My parents did the best they could, living paycheque to paycheque, but my mother recently told me she'd been in the dark about their financial situation. She just knew it wasn't good (which certainly sheds some light on my own need to be in financial control). Only after she and my father split up, when I was 13, did my mom write her first cheque.

I remember feeling really ashamed when my parents' marriage ended. I was the only kid in my class from a "broken family," and the other kids teased me about it. That made me believe that I was broken, too, and in high school, I felt as though I just didn't fit anywhere. I was so upset with my parents, wondering how they could've done this to me. I felt displaced and a little shell-shocked, and I never really regained my balance. I became an undisciplined student, coasting along without bothering to study most of the time. Ironically, my skipping a few years of grade school convinced me that I wasn't very smart; I was so much younger and less mature than my classmates that I always felt inferior to them. I did fine in some subjects—English, social studies—but flunked math several times. It didn't particularly bother me. I knew I would never have any need for math! My main memories of high school are of feeling not good enough and wanting to fly beneath the radar so no one else would notice. I'd be surprised if many of my classmates even remembered me. Here's how big an impression I made: in my high school yearbook, I was named most likely to be a candlestick maker, of all things.

When I graduated I was 16 years old, my mother was selling our house, and I felt I didn't have anywhere to go. I was just too immature to figure out how to get a loan or some funding to go to university, and besides, I'd convinced myself I wasn't university material. So I moved out on my own and got a job. My sole ambition in life was to get married and create the happy family I craved.

My father was devastated. He really believed education was everything; his whole life was about learning. He told me many times that I couldn't rely on a man, but without a degree, I would have no other choice: "You have to be able to take care of yourself, Arlene. It's your responsibility."

A teenager with a Mormon upbringing, I just didn't agree. There's a lot I still admire and respect about the church, years after leaving it, but it's a very patriarchal religion. At that time anyway, Mormons didn't frown on marrying young, though they sure did frown on premarital sex; one result was that a lot of girls wound up marrying their first serious boyfriends. I'd completely absorbed the message that my mission in life as a woman was to have children. So at 19, I got married to my best friend's brother. Their family belonged to our church, and I'd persuaded myself I wanted that Molly Mormon life: having a lot of kids, making a happy home. I wanted to create the kind of stability I'd never had as a child.

I had my first baby at 21, and by 27, I was raising four kids. We struggled financially—my husband went to university full time, studying to become a teacher, while I worked to support us all. We'd moved from Calgary to a small town 40 kilometres away, where we built our own home because we couldn't afford to buy one. I figured out how to use a hammer, put on roofing tiles (while I was seven months' pregnant), lay carpet, and hang wallpaper, all while managing a busy household and working at entry-level jobs.

I was busy trying to be the perfect mom, growing vegetables, canning, pickling, going to church. I didn't have a lot of time for reflection, which suited me fine, since reflection was uncomfortable. If I'd truly reflected on my circumstances, I'd have had to admit that I was living the life I'd thought I wanted, yet I was miserable. I adored my children and loved being a mother. But I didn't feel loved or appreciated by my husband, and I'd become convinced that this was *my* problem, that I simply wasn't smart enough or attractive enough or a good enough person to be worthy of love. My existence had narrowed to a single point: trying to please him and win his approval. And failing. To say I felt bad about myself would be putting it mildly. Every day, a litany of invalidations ran through my head, and it went something like this: you're dumb, uneducated, unlovable, unattractive, not good at anything.

I'm not proud of what happened next, but it was a pivotal point in my life so I need to be honest about it. When I was 30, I had an affair. I was so hungry for attention and validation that I didn't care where it came from. That's an explanation, not an excuse, and here's another: I lacked the courage to exit my marriage directly, the way I should have.

That affair turned out to be a life-changing event in many ways. For one thing, I learned that the whole Molly Mormon image I'd been striving for simply did not fit, and in any event, when my infidelity became known, I was excommunicated from my church (an agonizing process that involved a meeting with the bishop and other elders, where I was questioned in great detail, then condemned—which was particularly painful because I felt I deserved it).

I also discovered that the cost of acting against your own principles is far, far higher than anything you could possibly gain by doing so. I'm not just talking about the guilt that accompanies moral compromise but how I felt about myself during the affair and especially afterward. The shame of having to admit to myself that I was in fact a liar was excruciating. And the relief of not having to lie anymore was huge; lying requires a tremendous amount of energy and effort, and none of it is productive. It doesn't create anything except more bad feelings. I never wanted to feel that way again. I never wanted to cause that kind of harm again.

But the price I paid went beyond a crisis of conscience. When my husband found out about the affair, he made it plain that I couldn't remain in our home and so I fled—setting the stage for him to argue that I'd abandoned my children. I ended up sleeping on my dad's couch in Calgary, but I was pretty confident that because I was the mom, I would be granted sole custody of the kids. So confident that I trusted my lawyer implicitly and didn't think strategically or trust my own instincts. My ex positioned himself as a stay-at-home dad looking to better himself and the lives of our children. The judge asked whether he'd ever harmed the kids. No, he never had. The ruling was that our kids should not be uprooted and moved from their home, their school, their friends. So they stayed with my ex in our house and I had joint custody.

When I protested that I had nowhere else to go but my dad's house, and in any event needed to be in Calgary to find work, the family court judge told me that if I wanted my kids full time, I needed to get a place to live and prove I could support them financially. Until then, they'd live with my ex and I could see them every other weekend. Shock, anguish, grief, remorse—those words don't even begin to cover how I felt. I remember weeping on my dad's couch for days.

Then one day he got fed up and said, "You can't let this define you or ruin your life. You need to get on with it." My dad was a great persuader (partly motivated, no doubt, by the fact that he and my stepmother wanted their couch back, ASAP). He helped me understand that this was the pivotal moment in my life, the moment that would determine what kind of future my kids had and what role I would play in it. I had no prospects—no idea, even, of what I was good at. But I was our only hope. If I gave up on myself, I was essentially giving up my kids for good. And there would be no one else to blame for my failure.

My sister-in-law worked at a TV station in Calgary, and she managed to get me an interview for a job selling ads. She'd been at the station a long time, so her introduction really meant something, and beyond just putting herself out there to get me the interview she prepped me extensively. The most important thing she told me, my biggest confidence booster, was that the station was desperate to find someone who could start right away. That was one requirement I could certainly meet.

I remember the interview very clearly, right down to the red dress with white stripes I wore and the stale smell of the air in the tiny room. My resumé was pretty thin—consisting mostly of general administrative experience—but I pointed out that I had had a bit of PR experience years before, albeit in a clerical role, when I'd worked in the PR/media relations department at the University of Calgary. And, I told the sales guy who interviewed me, I wasn't a complete novice when it came to sales: my sister-in-law and I had started a gift basket company the year before.

He knew my hard-luck story, which indicated not only that I'd be motivated but that I could work round the clock, if necessary, since my kids weren't yet living with me. Plus, since I'd be working on commission, the downside to hiring me was fairly small. Still, I was surprised and frankly overjoyed when the station decided to take a chance on me.

Of course, I had no clue what I was doing, and I was scared to death in my first meetings with clients. But I had the good fortune to be teamed with a pro, an expert salesman who knew television advertising inside out. I very quickly discovered that slickness and media savvy weren't really what mattered, and that a hard sell didn't work. The most important thing was hearing and absorbing what the clients wanted, then explaining how buying an ad could help them achieve their business goals. There was no genius to it. It was just common sense, not that different from persuading my kids to do their homework. I turned out to be good at selling ads, really good. However, story of my life, I was let go from the TV station; I think management figured they could put someone on salary for less than I was making on commission.

My connection with the expert salesman turned out to be my saving grace. He had left the station to join a few partners in starting Venture. I'd met the group before and so when I left the station, they knew what I was capable of and offered me a job. It was a big risk. I could've looked for something more stable than Venture, which was still in the start-up phase, meaning a decent salary (or any salary) was out of the question. But I liked the idea of getting in on the ground floor. I was excited to learn more about marketing—I wasn't even sure exactly what it was, though I suspected it was really just a fancy way of saying "advertising"—and to help build a company I'd own part of, thanks to sweat equity. And I was honoured: the four other partners, all men, were older than me and had decades of professional experience. Yet they thought I merited a place at their table. I was going to be a partner! Of course, a title was an easy thing for them to give me; everyone who worked at Venture at that point was a partner.

And they knew that in return, I was going to try to bring in some of my clients from the TV station—and work my tail off.

And that is how, one year after my divorce, I came to be a partner at Venture. Several years later, when my children had a say in the matter, they chose to live with me. Getting them back was one of the happiest times of my life. Ten years after that conversation with my father, I bought out the one other remaining partner and became CEO of Venture. Today, 23 years after I got up off my dad's couch, I'm also a venture capitalist on a TV show, helping to fund other people's dreams. Even I can hardly believe the unlikely trajectory of my life.

But it wasn't an overnight success story. It was a long, hard slog, for years, and I've made mistakes—huge ones—along the way. I got through because I owned them, and learned from them, and also learned to own my past. Another thing I learned: our past shapes and influences who we are, but it doesn't limit who we can become.

The take-away? You don't need to tell others your life story to establish authenticity. But you do need to be honest with yourself, take responsibility for your choices, and own your weaknesses as well as your strengths. When people feel they're dealing with a real person who isn't hiding behind excuses or a mask, who's presenting a face to the world that's genuine, they know they're dealing with someone they can trust.

WHAT CHARACTER HAS TO DO WITH PERSUASION

Persuasion is active. Whether you're pitching for a new job or pitching City Hall to create a dog park in your neighbourhood, you're trying to get others to see things your way and to help you execute. Often you'll meet resistance, and sometimes you'll need to push people fairly hard to get them to sign on as partners. And then there are the blind alleys you'll hit, which will force you to find another path to get you to where you want to go. All of this requires serious determination on your part—you really have to believe your way is the right way—and absolute trust on the other person's part.

Your character is a huge part of what makes you trustworthy. And authenticity is the *sine qua non* of character. If you try to pretend you're someone you're not in order to get what you want, you'll be discovered, probably sooner rather than later. People can usually tell pretty quickly when they're dealing with a fake. So you have to stick with who you really are. At the end of the day, being true to yourself and honest with others is the only way to create the trust that's necessary for principled persuasion.

CHAPTER THREE

Honesty

A uthenticity is about being true to yourself. Honesty is about being truthful with others, and everyone knows it's the best policy. Right? Wrong. Honesty feels and actually can be dangerous in a lot of situations, especially when it requires speaking truth to power, taking a stand that might be unpopular, or revealing something about yourself or others that isn't entirely positive.

In an audition situation—a job interview, an initial meeting with the volunteer board you'd like to join—honesty can feel particularly risky. You want to seal the deal, not raise something that will give the other party pause, like the fact that you were fired from your last job or that your research has turned up some dirt on the other party. In ongoing relationships, too, sometimes shading the truth or lying by omission just feels more comfortable. Who wants to be the person to tell the boss that she's just plain wrong? Or to tell the PTA that the invitations to the school fundraiser cost $300 more than you said they would—and they've already been printed? Or to inform clients that one of your co-workers plagiarized some text that's now proudly displayed on their website? It might feel easier simply to fix the problem yourself, quietly, without ever bringing it to anyone's attention.

But the risk that something will be discovered after the fact and you'll appear to have been concealing information is just not worth taking. The damage to your reputation, and consequently your ability to persuade others, could be irreparable. Trust is the bedrock of ethical persuasion; the other party has to believe completely that you have told and always will tell the truth, even when it's difficult. When you persuade others to do something, by definition you have to overcome some resistance; either the path doesn't initially seem like the right one to them, or you don't seem to be the right partner, or the cost or method or strategy is one they're not initially convinced is right. So getting people to do things your way often means talking them out of a preconceived notion and asking them to take a leap of faith. To do that, they need to be able to rely on you completely. Once someone puts that kind of trust in you, the discovery of even a minor evasion or deception can be interpreted as a wholesale betrayal. This is why honesty is always the better choice, even when it requires sticking your neck out and risking your own head.

Never forget that whatever you do for a living, you're playing a long game, and your reputation is your most valuable asset. A loss today could turn into a win tomorrow or a year down the road so long as you've conducted yourself ethically. People remember honesty. More than once, Venture has bid for business with a pitch that was a little too honest for the prospective client's liking. The client wanted us to say we could do the work more cheaply or more quickly than we actually believed we could, and we didn't land the account. Months or even years later, some of these clients have come back, having been burned by agencies that overpromised and couldn't deliver, and said, "Still interested in working with us?" Long term, honesty isn't just the best policy. It's also the most persuasive one.

FIRST, FIGURE OUT WHICH LINES YOU WILL NOT CROSS

Although persuasion is a dynamic personal interaction and therefore never exactly the same twice, the principles behind it are simple and don't change. Benefits shouldn't be one-sided or lopsided. The methods shouldn't involve ruses or tricks—or, it should go without saying (but I'll say it anyway), anything illegal. There shouldn't be any wild promises that can't possibly be fulfilled.

Sometimes, however, you'll be tempted to throw these principles out the window because what's at stake—an amazing promotion, a huge amount of money—is something you want so much you'd do just about anything to get it. Other times, the consequences of failing to persuade seem so dire ("If I don't land this client I may lose my job and have to go live in my parents' basement"), you want to avoid them at all costs. Greed and desperation are the enemies of principled persuasion because when you want or need something too much, it can cloud your judgment. You may feel tempted to grab as much for yourself as you possibly can, especially if the other party doesn't resist. Or you may overpromise in order to clinch the deal and then be unable to deliver.

Which is why, long before you ever find yourself in such a situation, you must be very clear in your mind what your values are. Everyone needs to have clearly drawn lines they will not cross, no matter what's on the other side. My clearest, brightest line is that I won't lie to get business. A prospective client once called to let me know he'd chosen to go with another firm, explaining, "The reason you didn't get the account, Arlene, is that when we asked if you personally would be working on it day to day, you said no. If you'd said yes, we would've gone with Venture." He sounded disappointed, but I know he would've been far more disappointed if I'd pulled a bait and switch. Even though the Venture team would have done a great job, saying yes to win the work would have been a good idea only short term; long term, the consequences would have been bad for everyone.

Honesty has cost me a few accounts. But on the plus side, I can sleep at night, and being honest has kept the door open for future relationships. When you shade the truth and then can't deliver, that door slams shut.

Of course, business isn't always black and white. When the boss flirts with you—playfully, there's no harassment—should you use it to your advantage? If a co-worker asks you to cover for her so she can duck out early, should you do it? There's a lot of grey in business, and if you don't know what your values are, you can find yourself living in that grey zone. And it will probably get bigger and bigger because you'll start compromising your integrity without even realizing you're doing it, then discover you're on a slippery slope and can't backtrack. If you agree to something questionable once, it's much harder to say no the next time.

When you find yourself in the grey zone, there's a really helpful exercise you can do to figure out which way to go. Just imagine that you're being filmed and the clip is going to wind up on YouTube. Then do the thing you could live with if that clip went viral. Frankly, I've learned over the years that if I even have to stop and ask myself whether something is right or wrong, I already know the answer: it's wrong. Just having to ask the question means I've got one foot in the grey zone.

That's a place you never want to be when you're trying to persuade someone to do something. The long-term risks to your reputation are too serious. So how can you be sure, when you're pitching, that your methods of persuasion are ethical? It's pretty simple, really. All you have to do is put yourself in the other person's shoes and ask yourself two questions: Does what you're proposing still seem fair? And, knowing everything you do, would *you* agree to it? These are hard questions to answer honestly when what hangs in the balance is something you really want. But answering them truthfully is the best way to be sure you don't go grey and compromise your values.

HONESTY ATTRACTS THE KIND OF PEOPLE YOU WANT TO WORK WITH

Although there is a risk of offending the other party, when you have the courage to tell hard truths, you establish credibility that just can't be won any other way. You're making it clear that you're not just in it for yourself. You're willing to risk displeasure because you care about what's right for the other party, not just about getting what you want. Of course, short term, it's easier to skirt tough issues and tell people what they want to hear. But ultimately, a straight shooter is in a far better position to earn trust and create a productive working relationship. (It's also a whole lot easier to hold your head high and feel good about what you do.)

For instance, Venture once pitched a chain that was losing market share. The chain's executives had been meeting with just about every agency under the sun, and we were one of the last. It was a huge piece of business for us, and we were prepared to do whatever it took to win it. But in our initial meeting, as I listened intently to the management team tell me about all the great things they'd done to try to turn the chain's situation around, I realized with a sinking feeling that they were only listening to each other talk—and that none of the other agencies pitching the account had wanted to tell them the truth about their business. The senior executives needed to understand why people were staying away in droves, which had nothing to do with lacklustre marketing.

So our team arranged a focus group where we asked customers to talk honestly about the company, and we taped the whole thing. We then went back to the management team and said, "We don't have mock ads or fancy pie charts about market segmentation. We're not here to flatter you into hiring us but to tell you the truth. We have something you need to hear, and it's going to be hard to listen to." Then we played the tape. It was brutal. People said they hated just about everything about the business. They said that they'd rather go just about anywhere else. Let me tell you, it wasn't easy to inflict this barrage of criticism on the senior executives, and I knew there was a good chance their response would be to send us packing. But I also knew there was no point in sugar-coating the research and wrapping it up prettily. If we had to soft-pedal from the start, there was no way we could actually deliver results down the road.

When the tape finished, the room was silent for a moment. A very long moment. Then one of the executives sat back and said quietly, "You know, no one's ever told us that before." Venture went on to enjoy a long and highly successful partnership with that chain; we were able to persuade them to take risks that helped turn their business around. They trusted us and respected our advice because we'd been truthful with them from the start, even at the risk of not landing the account in the first place.

In audition situations where you really want the job or the business or the opportunity, honesty immediately establishes your ethics. People who find this unattractive or inconvenient or impertinent are not people you want to work with or for. If you have to shade the truth from the outset, it's not possible to establish a reciprocal relationship that will be rewarding to both of you. And at some point, it will lead to trouble. There's always a day of reckoning, so I figure, why not make it the very first one?

When you're truthful at the outset, there are no nasty surprises down the road. I recently pitched to a major multinational manufacturer whose Canadian leader had some impressive goals for what he wanted to achieve in this country, and a clear idea of exactly what he wanted to spend. He named the figure and I said, "We're probably not the right agency for you—I'm not going to lie to you and pretend I can do everything you want for the dollar amount you just named. I'm not going to take your money just because you're prepared to spend it." He was surprised; no other agency had said the budget was too low. That's right, I thought, they'd rather land the account, then break it to you a few months on, when the money is all gone. I gave him a few detailed examples of what other corporations spend to achieve the same types of goals—between six and seven times the amount he'd mentioned. His response was "Okay, that's fair. And I hope you'll submit a proposal because I think you might be the right agency." I don't know if we'll land the account, but I do know that the possibility of a positive working relationship exists because there's already trust on both sides.

WHEN YOU DON'T KNOW, SAY SO

When you're trying to persuade someone, it might not feel safe to admit that you don't know or don't understand something. Especially in an audition situation, like pitching a new client or presenting an idea to the powers that be at work, a lot of people are afraid to ask questions because they don't want to look ignorant. But although saying nothing may seem less embarrassing, it's not more persuasive. In fact, being willing to admit that you don't know something is usually read as confidence. Better than 9 times out of 10, the interpretation of

"I probably should know this, but I don't—what does *x* mean?" will not be that you're a dolt but that you're secure enough and intelligent enough to want to be able to follow and contribute to the conversation. Plus, you're interested in learning. Trust me, someone who's on the up and up will not make you feel like an idiot if you ask, "What does that mean, exactly?"

And no, I'm not just saying that because I so frequently find myself admitting that I don't know something. I'm saying it because the alternative is bluffing. Unless you're a practised liar, when you bluff, you will likely telegraph signals that others might pick up on. Even if they don't figure out exactly what it is that you don't know, they could well sense instinctively that something's not quite right— and that could sink your pitch, no matter how strong it is. Occasionally on *Dragons' Den,* I've been on the verge of offering a deal to an entrepreneur, then sensed something inauthentic. I back off immediately, even if I can't pinpoint exactly what the problem might be.

And, of course, when you bluff, you also risk being caught out, which really *is* embarrassing. You know exactly what I'm talking about if you've ever been in the awkward situation of not being familiar with a phrase or concept or a name that seems to trip off everyone else's tongue, but the conversation has progressed so far that it no longer feels possible to admit it. Then you're asked, straight out, for your opinion or decision—and you have to confess you have no clue.

So don't let insider lingo or impenetrable acronyms scare you into silence. Chances are good that the concepts dressed up in fancy jargon are ones you can grasp pretty easily. For instance, I often meet senior executives who've been hoodwinked into thinking marketing is some baffling form of voodoo they could never hope to understand. But, in fact, marketing is very simple. It's all about taking your business to the market, and making sure people know and understand what is unique and compelling about doing business with you.

Far from knocking you out of the running, sometimes simply admitting that you don't know something can create the first spark of emotional connection that underpins persuasion. Your honesty establishes that you're human and confident—a pretty appealing combination. And if honesty *isn't* appealing to the other party, that's important information to have.

A WHITE LIE CAN CREATE AN INDELIBLE STAIN ON YOUR REPUTATION

Just as people remember honesty, they also remember dishonesty. Even what seems like a minor fib can wind up causing major damage to your reputation. Calling in sick so you can go golfing may seem like a white lie, but if you're caught, it might not be. It could turn into a referendum on your character, in the same way that a politician caught stretching the truth even a little bit often winds up being viewed thereafter as untrustworthy and unelectable.

I find it really troubling when someone I work with is not truthful with me. It causes a permanent rift in the emotional connection, even when the lie is minor. One interesting example from a few years ago involved what some people at my company viewed as a white lie. Here's what happened: I made a decision a long time ago that employees shouldn't have to work on their birthdays. If yours falls on a weekday, you get the day off. Happy birthday! However, if your birthday falls on a weekend, you've already got the day off, so you don't need to have a weekday off too. Having a weekend birthday could be viewed as bad luck, or as an incentive to continue working for Venture, since eventually your birthday *will* fall on a weekday. Well, one employee questioned the policy and said it really wasn't fair. He argued that it was essentially punitive to people

69

whose birthdays fell on the weekend. I explained that the intent was to ensure that no one had to come into the office on his or her birthday, not that everyone at Venture gets an extra day off every year.

A while later, this employee told his manager that the next day was his birthday, and on that day, he didn't come into the office. My gut instinct was that he was not telling the truth, and there was an easy way to find out, as all birthdays are noted on our intranet. So I checked, and sure enough, it revealed that this guy had gone into the system and manually changed his date of birth earlier in the week. So I fired him. Did I overreact? Some people at the company thought so.

But to me, the issue was black and white: he knowingly broke our policy and altered records. Someone who could do this was too comfortable in the grey zone for my liking, and not someone I could ever be persuaded to trust again. I had to consider the liability for the company if he ever altered records or lied to a client. Now, maybe he never would've done anything like that. But I'd never know for sure. And as a business owner, you just can't afford to take a chance on an employee's integrity.

My point here is that, like beauty, dishonesty is in the eye of the beholder. I'm sure this guy really thought that what he was doing was no big deal, but I saw things differently. You just can't count on the way someone else will interpret it when you shade the truth, or what the reaction will be. Which is why the best course is always the straightest and narrowest one, where there is no room for misunderstanding.

IF YOU TRY TO FAKE IT UNTIL YOU MAKE IT, YOU MAY SHOOT YOURSELF IN THE FOOT

Honesty compels me at this point to tell a story on myself, about a time when I tried to make a good impression but wound up doing the opposite. A few years ago, Venture reached the final round of bidding for a U.S. corporation that was seeking help to create and deploy a brand strategy. I'd had several meetings already with the senior executives, and in this final meeting needed to present a detailed marketing plan. At that time, we were in the process of expanding our business and opening a Toronto office; I'd hired someone who would be the linchpin of that office—let's call him "Mark"—but he wasn't scheduled to start for another week.

Nevertheless, a day or so before we were scheduled to do our final pitch, I decided Mark should join us, since, if we won the account, he'd be helping to manage it day to day. So I asked him to fly down to the States for the pitch along with me and Jennifer Cioffi, who'd only recently joined Venture herself (and is today president of the company). Shortly before our flight, I realized that Mark didn't even have a Venture business card yet, so I called our print production manager and asked him to print up a few and FedEx them to us. Well, it just wasn't possible in that short time frame, but he's a genius at this sort of thing and did manage to cobble together something by gluing a new front to an existing, shaved-down Venture card. It looked completely professional, though it was kind of thick, and he only had time to make a few of them.

The next day, the three of us huddled in the hotel restaurant, poring over the marketing plan, which was largely Jen's creation. It was her first Venture pitch ever and Mark's introduction to our company, so we were in overdrive, tossing ideas back and forth, strategizing about the client—everything you normally do before a presentation, just compressed into a very short period with a team of three people who didn't know each other well at all. Luckily, the restaurant was one of those half-empty places you find only in the American South, where the staff is super friendly and will let you sit there forever, happily pouring you cup after cup of bad coffee.

After wrapping up, we asked the woman at the front desk for directions to the corporation's headquarters and were told it was just a short distance away, across a sprawling research park. We set off and pretty soon had no idea where we were going. Every building looked the same, and some had no signage or numbers, so one of us would have to run up to the front door to find out if it was the right place. It was hot and I was in heels, but I'm a fast walker, so I took the lead. Jen tells this story better than I do, and when she gets to this point she always says, "I'm basically trotting along behind Arlene, soaked in sweat, thinking, 'Maybe coming to Venture was a bad career move.'" We couldn't find the building, so eventually I had to call the client contact, describe what I could see around us, and get her to guide us to the building.

We finally arrived, late and dripping wet. But the vice-president was all Southern charm when we showed up panting, and said, "Oh, you're the people from the restaurant!" We were mortified. She'd been sitting at the table next to us and had doubtless heard us scrambling and brainstorming.

But there was nothing else to do but mop our foreheads, hand out our business cards, and pitch. Jen took the lead, as this was really her baby. Now, I should tell you that Jen is a perfectionist and highly persuasive, but she had never done a pitch before and was a little rattled by everything that had happened to that point. Because we were late arriving she went a mile a minute, reeling off at a dizzying pace all the things we were going to do for the company. The instant she finished, our new VP Mark turned to her and declared in his big, booming voice, "Well, my goodness, I think that's the most amazing plan I have ever seen in my life! Just amazing." As though he'd never clapped eyes on it (which was not far from the truth, really). Jen looked totally confused, and I could tell she was thinking, "Okay, maybe this is what happens in a pitch." Then at that moment, she and

I noticed that the client was playing with Mark's business card, bending it back and forth with a quizzical expression on her face. Then the VP said, "Hmm. This card is *crunchier* than the others." While Mark went on about how stunning Jen's work was, how he just could not get over it, Jen and I watched in agony as the VP bent his card. I could hear it cracking, about to fall apart. Finally the VP asked Mark, "So, how long have you been at Venture?"

Which is when I said what I should have said at the very beginning of the meeting, along with explaining that he didn't yet have a business card: "He's officially starting next week, but I wanted to make sure you met him, as he would be the Toronto point person on this project."

In the end, we did not win the account, but we did take the lesson. When you posture, you run the risk of embarrassing yourself. And of not persuading anyone. The truth is, I took Mark with us because I was serious and enthusiastic about getting the work, but by omitting to mention that he was brand new, I may have created the opposite impression.

In general, if you try to gloss over what you view as a shortfall—a gap in your resumé, a lack of expertise in a certain area—you may create a problem where none existed before. Being anything less than upfront is just plain foolish because you can wind up looking less than trustworthy, even when you haven't done anything dishonest.

FULL DISCLOSURE IS THE SMARTEST POLICY

Sometimes, entrepreneurs on *Dragons' Den* fail to disclose something negative that surfaces later, when it can be interpreted as a lie of omission and wind up killing a deal. For instance, right after one episode aired, a stranger called me out of the blue to say, "You should know I'm suing the entrepreneur you did a deal with last night." The entrepreneur's rebuttal was "My lawyer told me I didn't need to tell you because the suit has no merit." Well, maybe not, but I was really perturbed to find out about a pending legal action this way. How could I trust someone who had tried to keep me in the dark? It would have been much better to say, "Look, there's an issue you should know about upfront. It amounts to nothing, but I did want you to hear about it from me first."

Whatever the issue is—being fired from a previous job, having what could be perceived as a conflict of interest—you want to be the one to disclose it. The simple act of taking the initiative to disclose a problem can have the effect of creating trust; you're admitting a vulnerability and proving that you're straightforward and have nothing to hide. Being open and transparent about the bad stuff, as well as the good, establishes your ethics. And your courage. Most people appreciate that it's most important to tell the truth when it's also the most difficult.

HONESTY SETS THE STAGE FOR RECIPROCITY

Authenticity is about telling the truth to yourself, so that you can make your character clear to others. Honesty is about telling the truth to others—and knowing that, sometimes, truth-tellers *don't* get the job or close the deal, but they do hang on to their reputations, which, long term, has to be tallied as a win. These are the aspects of character and ethics that promote the emotional connection that's key to persuasion.

The third key aspect concerns your strategic ability and your understanding of the need to construct every proposition so that it has something in it not just for you but also for the other party. If you're authentic and honest, you've proven you're a good person, but if reciprocity is not part of each deal, you won't be a good persuader.

CHAPTER FOUR

Reciprocity

When I started in business, I was stunned the first time I saw someone trick people into buying overpriced services they didn't need. I remember thinking, "Wow, *that's* salesmanship." I knew I could never pull that off, and wondered if I was really cut out for the business world. Over the years, I've seen a lot more people use trickery to do everything from influencing board votes to getting others to sign questionable deals, and now I think, "Wow, that's so slimy. Thank God I was never able to do it."

When I'm pitching for new business or trying to change a client's or colleague's mind about something, I need to believe the other person will benefit. If *I* don't believe it, I can't persuade anyone else. To me, persuasion is a bit evangelical. You must have faith that the path you're advocating is right for the other person. And you have to be able to spell out very clearly and succinctly why it's in their best interests.

Of course, when you persuade, you want to get something out of it too. You're not being altruistic. If, for instance, you're trying to convince your kids' school to cut back a bit on homework, the purpose isn't to make teachers' lives easier—your main goal is to ensure your children aren't spending every spare moment on schoolwork. And the best way to achieve it is not to trick or trap the other side but to show them how this would be a win for them too.

In this chapter, we'll look at ways to be sure you're building reciprocity into every pitch. I'll explain how a power differential can affect a pitch, and what you need to do to ensure you're appealing to those you're trying to persuade, whether they have more, less, or about the same amount of power as you do.

QUESTIONS TO ASK YOURSELF

Before you start trying to persuade people, ask yourself, What's in it for them? Is this something they really need or can use? If not, how can I build in more benefits for them? Does it help me more than it helps them? What might I lose if I don't persuade them? What might they lose?

Thinking through these questions beforehand is especially important when you're pitching to someone you've never met before. If there's no shared history or past experience, you're starting from ground zero in terms of creating an emotional connection. Typically, the other person is going to be a little more wary and also probably a little less willing to give you the benefit of the doubt if you trip up in some way.

If there's no pre-existing relationship, you will probably also have less time to establish that you've got something of value to offer. On the show, for instance, the average pitch lasts about 25 minutes (they're edited before they're aired). But entrepreneurs only have about two minutes at most to persuade us their business is worth investing in, and that they are capable leaders. After that I'm still listening, but I've already decided whether I have confidence in the entrepreneur's idea and ability to run a business. If I'm not persuaded after the first minute or so, there's rarely any hope of changing my mind. I don't think I'm unusual in this regard. Think of how quickly you decide whether you want to keep watching a TV show or continue talking to someone at a party.

In many real-life situations—a bid for new business, an interview for a graduate program, a pitch to seek a zoning change in your neighbourhood—the window of opportunity for persuasion is very narrow. In Part IV, we'll look at all the ways to make the best use of the time you have, but the first step is to have the conceptual framework of persuasion clear in your mind: you need to be both authentic and honest, and your pitch must stress, above all, what's in it for the other party.

This is true regardless of the power dynamic in any particular situation. Sometimes you'll be pitching up to people who have more power—or higher social status. And sometimes you'll be the most powerful person in the room, pitching down to juniors—or to, say, the babysitter, who depends on the wages you pay. Sometimes (and this can be most tricky) you're pitching sideways, to peers and co-workers, siblings and friends. But whether you're pitching to a manager, an intern, or a colleague, a VIP, a teenager, or your sister, you should be able to explain exactly how the other person stands to benefit. And the better you know that person, the more you will be expected to understand and articulate the impact on him of whatever it is you're proposing.

PITCHING WHEN YOU HAVE LESS POWER

I started my work life in entry-level clerical positions, and I've made stops at just about every rung on the career ladder. Along the way, I've had the opportunity to see the business world from many vantage points. One thing I've learned is that people do treat you differently depending on your position on the ladder, which is why it's so important to hang on to your sense of yourself and be true to your values, regardless of where you stand. To remain grounded, your sense of your own worth has to come from within, not from others.

When you're perceived to have more power, you will sometimes get preferential treatment—but you will also, on some occasions, be treated with less consideration. For example, the notion of reciprocity sometimes goes right out the window when people are pitching to higher-ups. It's like a teenager who forgets, when he's angling for something, to point out what could possibly be in it for you as a parent. Some pitchers simply feel they don't need to offer benefits to those who already have more than they do. The thinking is "They've got so much, why would they need anything else?" Or, "They've reached a point in their careers where they're going to be benevolent." The other day, for instance, I got an email from a teenager asking me to send him money so he could buy a car. I have a soft heart, but not that soft. A demand for money or help or time, with nothing in it for me or the greater good of humankind, just doesn't work. Sitting through something like 1,500 pitches so far on *Dragons' Den* has toughened me up a little, in a good way. I've been taken enough times now that a sob story just doesn't work quite as well as it used to. It's funny how many people don't even bother to work up a story, they just come on set and blurt out something like "I've got kids, too" and think that's going to be the right chord to get me to open my wallet.

Here's the thing you need to understand when pitching up: people who make it to the top may have even *higher* expectations from a pitch. Maybe it's because they're in a position to do more for you than others could. Or maybe it's because they had to work so hard to get where they are and expect others to do the same. Or maybe it's that more people are trying to persuade them to do things, so their bullshit meters are more sensitive. Whatever the case, in my experience, senior business people are more likely to be jaded cynics, since they've usually had more experience of deals going south. What they're looking for is tangible evidence that you can deliver, and like everyone else, they want to know what's in it for them.

However, some pitchers simply forget to describe the benefits they're offering. We see this a fair bit on *Dragons' Den*. Some entrepreneurs stress how much they need our help to achieve their dreams but fail to mention what the advantage would be to us. No matter how smooth your delivery and how much you deserve success, if you don't focus on what you have to offer the other party and why it's good for them too—forget it. You sound like you're looking for charity, not partners.

Why do people do this when pitching up? Occasionally, the problem is a sense of entitlement. Some people just feel they deserve success and shouldn't have to do anything much to achieve it. Generally, though, I think people get flustered by a power imbalance and the stress of the situation. I think they forget about reciprocity when pitching to higher-ups because they feel inferior rather than like equals who just happen to have less power in the particular situation. Sometimes on the show, for instance, I feel pitchers aren't trying to persuade us, really. They're trying to impress the TV stars they imagine we are, rather than trying to convince the five relatively normal people who are actually sitting in front of them. They're boxing with shadows, in other words.

Having less power doesn't mean you are of lesser worth and therefore don't have anything to offer. It's crucial to remember this when the stakes are high and another person has the ability to grant what you desire. As soon as you focus on a real or perceived power imbalance rather than on what you bring to the table, you risk forfeiting the very real power you do have: the power to persuade.

Don't inflate the other person's importance

There's a tendency to attribute magical skills and knowledge to people who've been elevated in some way—appearing on TV, or having an impressive title, or coming from a wealthy family. There's often an assumption that these people possess some rare, mysterious qualities mere mortals lack. What crap.

Having spent the first 50 years of my life able to go into a grocery store without being recognized (or even noticed, frankly), I find it a little surreal to be on the receiving end of this way of thinking. Almost as soon as I joined *Dragons' Den,* strangers began treating me differently, as though by virtue of appearing on a reality TV show I'd morphed into an infallible sage (naturally, my kids and just about everyone else who knows me found this hilarious). Of course, I'm the same person I've always been, so I *really* know what a mistake it is to exaggerate and inflate other people's abilities simply because of their title or public profile or social position.

The worst part is that you run the risk of diminishing your sense of self-worth. Aside from all the other ways this can mess up your life, it's deadly in a persuasion situation. Especially when you're asking for help or backing, you can't put the other party on a pedestal and position yourself at the base, looking up hopefully for a favour. Along with a lack of confidence, you're essentially signalling that you don't really believe you deserve whatever it is you're asking for. Think, for instance, of the way some people bow and scrape for bank loans, as though they're asking for interest-free gifts, when in fact, over the long term, they'll help the bank make money. People are at their most convincing when they understand and communicate, respectfully but with absolute clarity, that they aren't just seeking help from on high— that they have something of value to offer.

PITCHING WHEN YOU HAVE MORE POWER

Reciprocity is also sometimes overlooked when the most senior person in the room is trying to persuade everyone else to do things her way. When executives are trying to get employees to work longer hours, for instance, or to embrace a whole new way of doing business, they often forget to spell out what's in it for the "little people." Sometimes the thinking is "What's in it for them? They'll get to keep their jobs is what!" If this were a truly persuasive argument, every troubled company in the world would be able to turn itself around on a dime and save a fortune on consultants. Employees would just put their noses to the grindstone and work furiously to keep their jobs—instead of shuffling back to their desks and resuming business as usual, which is exactly what tends to happen when they haven't been convinced of the need to change.

Persuading people to change the way they do their work requires that you spell out what's in it for them, especially if the benefit won't be immediate or even short term. Before you even attempt this, it's very helpful to try to put yourself in their shoes. How motivated would you feel if someone told you that in return for working like a dog, you would get—why, nothing more than what you already have today! How happy would you be if you were informed that you had to come in on the weekend in order to help move to a new office—in exchange for no extra time off!

Of course, sometimes a manager can't offer the promise of more money or a promotion or even an extra day off. Sometimes the only thing a higher-up can offer in the way of reciprocity is a commitment that she, too, will change the way she does her job. Maybe that means giving up a perk or getting her own coffee. Or making the coffee. Maybe it means consciously offering more recognition when people are doing a great job or taking more time to celebrate successes.

81

Maybe it means ordering pizza when everyone's working late. There are all kinds of ways to make people's work lives better when more is being demanded of them. And little things can be game changers in terms of office morale and corporate culture.

For instance, at Venture we have a Thursday afternoon ritual. We close our offices in Calgary and Toronto at 4 p.m., and people gather in the kitchen for what we call "Beers and Cheers." It's a great way to let people blow off some steam and celebrate what went well that week, and it helps foster the personal relationships that are key when times get tough. We don't ask people to stay late to socialize. It's a relatively inexpensive way for me to signal both gratitude and the importance of knowing your co-workers as people, not just colleagues, by ensuring that socializing occurs during office hours.

In both of our offices, one person had been in charge of buying food and drinks for this event for years now. But as our business has expanded and all of our schedules have become crazier, it recently became obvious that having to run out to the store every Thursday to stock up on snacks and drinks was too much for one person to shoulder. I wanted to ask people to help, but I knew if I said, "This is everyone's job," there would be a rebellion. I had to find a way to make it win-win. So I sent out a group email announcing Venture's next great chef contest: contestants will have the same budget and a bit of time off on Thursday to prepare whatever they've decided to make for Beers and Cheers—and the winner of the contest will get extra time off on the long weekend of his or her choice. A ton of people volunteered to compete and now the burden of prepping is shared between all of us. This is a pretty simple solution that will cost me about the same as Thursday's event has always cost me, and it benefits everyone.

One thing I've learned over the years is that if you present a de facto decision and say, "Buy in," people tend to nod their heads, then go do what they want. Everyone wants to feel included and that they've had input into any process that has a direct impact on their work lives. As part of the persuasion process, then, it's crucial to listen to the people who are stakeholders in the outcome of whatever process you're trying to change. Now, you may not wind up taking their advice, but you can explain clearly why not, and the outcome is likely to be better understanding on both sides. For instance, a few years ago, some people in our Toronto office asked if Beers and Cheers could be moved to Friday and renamed "Funnel Fridays." I listened to their reasons—business is winding down around 4 o'clock anyway at the end of the work week, and people are getting ready to go out on the town—but decided against it. Our tradition isn't meant to kick off a night of partying; it's about having a sociable drink—or cup of tea—with colleagues and hearing what they've been up to before heading home for the night.

This exchange was helpful, as it forced me to clarify not just for others but for myself exactly what the purpose of the event is, and people in the Toronto office felt I'd considered their proposal. It's easier for people to accept a "no" if they've been able to have a say, and if they feel you've listened and understood their perspective even though you don't agree with it. This, too, is a form of reciprocity: listening closely, regardless of how much power a person has.

To be clear, I'm not saying that the most powerful person in the room needs to seek consensus in order to persuade, particularly if the issue under discussion touches on overall business strategy. The truth is, you don't build a company through consensus. You build it through allowing people to feel they can collaborate and contribute, but they need to understand *what* they're collaborating on or contributing to, and that vision is developed by a small group of core individuals who have skin in the game. The guy in the mailroom shouldn't have a say in long-term strategy. He may be gone next week. But you should listen to what he thinks about his job and any ideas he has on improving his performance or productivity in his department. And you should certainly treat him with respect. And you never know, he might just be your boss one day.

In every situation where there's a power differential—with your children, for instance, or your cleaner—you need to think about reciprocity before you pitch. The fact that you have more power or more status or more money doesn't mean that you need cooperation and buy-in any less. At the end of the day, you're still looking for the same thing everyone looks for in any persuasion situation: agreement. And getting to yes is always easier if you can demonstrate that you understand the impact on and benefits to the other person.

PITCHING TO PEERS

In most work environments, persuading colleagues is something you're doing all day long. "Could you watch the cash while I grab lunch?" "I'm supposed to get this report finished by the end of the day, can you help me out with the statistical analysis?" And so on.

Often reciprocity is unstated but implied: Next time you need help, I'll be there for you. This is where it's clear that an emotional connection is a huge plus in persuasion. A co-worker's willingness to help depends largely on your relationship to date. If she thinks you're a genuine person who reciprocates favours, the answer will probably be yes. If she thinks you're a mooch, she'll try to find a way to get out of doing whatever it is you want her to do. Or she'll do a sub-par job.

In the 20-odd years I've been in marketing, I've had a close-up view of the inner workings and office politics of a wide range of companies and organizations. Almost always, the people who have the most influence with their peers, the ones who are really good persuaders, are the most collaborative and inclusive. They readily share credit for successes and take personal responsibility for failures. They may not have the biggest paycheques or best titles, but they are the most widely respected, and they can leverage that goodwill when they need to persuade co-workers and managers.

The thought leaders in any work environment almost always view business as a team sport. They know a goal isn't scored just by the centre but also by the defence and everyone else who assists. Your everyday conduct, then, is key to persuading colleagues in specific situations. If you're a team player, you imply reciprocity in everything you do—it's already part of your personal brand. That's why other people will listen and really consider what you have to say when you're seeking backing for an idea or a process.

THE ESSENTIALS

Authenticity, honesty with others, the promise of reciprocity—these three elements are the foundation of principled persuasion, not just in business but also the rest of life. These elements have everything to do with ethics, obviously, but also with self-awareness and self-confidence. You have to know—and accept—who you are, your flaws as well as your strengths, in order to communicate most effectively with others. Remember, authenticity is a powerful source of personal authority and far more likely to inspire others' trust than posturing or posing ever could. You have to have self-confidence to be willing to risk honesty, as telling hard truths can be uncomfortable and can sometimes even feel dangerous. But honesty is worth any risk because it's what allows others to trust you, and trust is what makes others want to partner with you. Finally, focusing on reciprocity—what's in it for them, not just for you—means having both the self-awareness to understand your impact on others and the self-assurance to seek true partners.

Many people who hold themselves to the highest ethical standards, and who wholeheartedly embrace the concepts of authenticity, honesty, and reciprocity in their dealings with others, nevertheless lack self-awareness and self-confidence. That's why they aren't very persuasive. How can you convince others to see things your way if you haven't persuaded yourself that you're worth paying attention to? The short answer is, you can't.

So before we can get down to the nitty-gritty details of the process involved in persuading others, we need to look at the art of self-persuasion, which begins with a clear-eyed assessment of the obstacles that stand between you and your goals. Chances are good that there's just one thing blocking your path: you.

PART THREE

SO, WHAT'S STANDING IN YOUR WAY?

To some people, success means making $10 million by the age of 40. To others, it means being an amazing parent while managing to hold down a part-time job. It could mean feeling excited about going to work every day, or believing you're making the world a better place, or having as many new experiences as possible, or having as many material comforts as possible. Everyone defines it a little differently.

What does success look like to you? And if you don't feel you've achieved it, what's standing in your way? Sometimes the obstacles are external; you haven't been able to line up reliable child care for your kids, say, or you work in an industry that was hit hard by the recession. But frequently, the most significant obstacles are internal and involve fear—of change, of failure, of humiliation.

Before you can persuade anyone else that you deserve a new job or a raise or a larger role or a new piece of work, you have to persuade yourself. This is the most important pitch you will ever make, and for many people, it's also the most difficult.

Which is not to say that most of us aren't good at self-persuasion. Quite the opposite. Self-persuasion is where many people really shine—so long as they're persuading themselves they *can't* do things. It comes naturally to the guy who can't stand his job but has convinced himself it's just not possible to get a better one. And to the student who's talked herself into believing she'd never get into law school. And to the CEO who has persuaded herself that changing her business model simply isn't feasible in this economy. Unfortunately, many people inadvertently use their talent for self-persuasion to deepen any rut they find themselves in and limit their chances of escaping.

A lot of us are amazingly good at convincing ourselves we can't possibly surmount the obstacles that stand between us and our goals: "Oh, I'll never get promoted, the boss just doesn't like me." "I don't think I'll ever own a home, I'm just not a saver." "Me, a fiftysomething woman with wrinkles, on *Dragons' Den*? No way. This isn't British television, after all."

Frequently, we're highly creative and resourceful when persuading ourselves we can't do things, capable of coming up with endless reasons to support the pitch: "I'd love to work outside the home, but I just can't. Yes, both kids are at school full time now, but I have to pick them up afterward, of course, then drive them to skating lessons, gymnastics, tutoring—besides, what would I do when they got sick? You can't just take weeks off work because your kids have colds. And it's been years since I set foot in an office; I'm just not up to date on all the software. I'd have to retrain, probably. Plus, I'd have to lose 15 pounds to fit into any of my old work clothes. Not that they're in style anymore—I'd need a whole new wardrobe, and you know how expensive that is. So you can see my problem. I'm desperate to get a job, but I'm trapped."

Of course, a talent for self-persuasion doesn't have to be a negative. For one thing, it's proof positive that you can be pretty persuasive when you want to be. For another, it's quite possible to convert a harsh inner critic into a fair and balanced reviewer. But to do that, you first need to recognize what negative self-talk is doing to you and how it's preventing you from succeeding. Inevitably, this requires thinking not just about your professional life but also about your personal life, your core beliefs about yourself and your place in the world. After all, when we walk in the office door, we don't check our emotional baggage. We bring it with us.

CHAPTER FIVE

Talking ourselves out of success

The soundtrack of most people's lives is an internal monologue consisting of things we say to ourselves throughout the day as we face problems and make decisions: "Do I turn left or right?" "I'm never going to finish this spreadsheet on time." "Come on, focus." It's stream of consciousness, and sometimes the volume is dialled down so low that you're not even wholly aware of it.

But even when you're not tuning in and listening closely, if the endless tape loop in your head is playing constant criticism—"Why did I just say something so dumb? No wonder I'm a failure"—it has a significant impact. Dwelling on what you see as your shortcomings— "I'm not skilled enough, not talented enough, not smart enough"— often makes them seem much more serious and disabling than they actually are. A lot of research shows that the more you chew over the bad stuff in your life and work, the worse you feel and the less able you are to solve your problems. Focusing on the negative saps your motivation to implement solutions even when they're readily available.

So you can wind up talking yourself into a state of paralysis. When an opportunity or new challenge presents itself, suddenly the volume of the background music is turned way up, and your response is automatic: "I can't do it, I'm not _____ enough." In this way, the internal monologue can become a self-fulfilling prophecy. You start by telling yourself you can't do something, and soon enough, you really *can't* do it. You're immobilized.

In this chapter, we'll look at what your self-talk is doing to you and how to change it from a destructive to a constructive force. I'll explain how thinking like an entrepreneur can help you move forward and overcome obstacles—especially the ones you've put in your own way.

THE GOOD THING ABOUT FEELING BAD

A negative internal monologue can be so compelling that you block out anything that contradicts it. For instance, for the first half of my life, I told myself I just wasn't very smart. There was evidence to the contrary: I'd figured out how to support myself at 16, and as a young mom strapped for cash, I'd learned how to do everything from growing vegetables to shingling a roof. But I ignored facts that didn't fit my theory.

Why? Well, strange as it seems to me now, I was pretty attached to my poor self-image. Feeling bad about myself didn't make me happy, but it was comfortable. It gave me the perfect excuse not to try things that scared me, like going to university. And there was another benefit: I didn't have to experience the discomfort of trying. Let's face it, attempting something new when you're not confident of success is really hard work. It's like skating for the first time. Other people glide past effortlessly, but you feel shaky and uncoordinated, afraid even to try to move because you just know you're going to fall. Plus, you know that everyone will see.

Self-talk of the I-can't-do-it variety, then, serves a self-protective purpose. If you tell yourself it's hopeless, there's no way you could ever get the promotion/quit smoking/start your own business—well, you're sparing yourself the hardship of trying, as well as the possibility of humiliation.

EXTERNAL OBSTACLES

Many times, obstacles to success are internal. People have persuaded themselves they just don't have what it takes. Other times, though, they're convinced the obstacles are external—the old boys' network, say, or an unfair boss, or a lack of funds, or a corporate culture that values experience over talent or youth over wisdom. In other words, they're confident about their abilities but believe they're being held back by forces they're powerless to control. Occasionally, this is true. Many people do work in organizations that are not meritocracies. Many people have experienced some form of discrimination in the workplace. Many corporate cultures grind people down rather than build them up.

Sometimes, however, the external barriers we perceive are far from insurmountable. Interestingly, although the moral of all North American rags-to-riches stories is that anyone can make it to the top, many people cling to the idea that the kind of lives they dream of are the birthright of a favoured few and out of reach of everyone else. People often shrug and say things like "If only my parents had had the money to send me to private school" or "If only I had an MBA," then trail off wistfully, as though the rest is clear.

But it isn't. There's no denying that starting out life with wealth and privilege gives you a significant advantage. But there's also no denying that many of the real superstars in this country, in all fields of endeavour, didn't begin their lives that way. They're self-made. Many of them got where they are today precisely because they *didn't* feel entitled to success and therefore committed themselves to working harder than everyone around them.

The truth is, you don't have to have a pedigree, or a degree from a particular university, or a certain accent or manner or skin colour or ethnicity to make it big in Canada. This is not to say that everyone can do—or is willing to do—what it takes to succeed. You need to have a well-developed skill set, an enormous appetite for hard work, an openness to opportunity, a willingness to learn, some common sense, and uncommonly good judgment. But our life stories don't have to be special and privileged in order for us to have meaningful and purposeful lives.

Potential, problems—we all have both.

PERSUADE YOURSELF THERE'S POTENTIAL IN WHATEVER PATH YOU'RE ON NOW

Virtually all entrepreneurs share one really valuable attribute: they see potential all around them. Often they zero in on a problem in their own lives and come to view it as a business opportunity. For instance, Sandra Wilson had been laid off from her job and was staying at home with her son when she noticed she couldn't find baby shoes that would stay on his feet. So she launched a company that sells soft-soled baby shoes that are elasticized around the ankle so they don't slip off. In 2006, she sold that company, Robeez, for $27.5 million.

Some entrepreneurs even view significant external obstacles as opportunities. For instance, during the depths of the recent recession, start-ups were launching virtually every day. These entrepreneurs looked at the economic picture and told themselves, "Large corporations are cutting back and holding off on decisions—that means there's room now for a smaller, more nimble company with lower overhead. I'm in."

I understand this way of thinking because it's how I view the world, too. The economic picture wasn't exactly rosy when I joined Venture in 1988. We were still experiencing the aftershocks of Black Monday, in October 1987; access to capital and forecasts for economic growth in Canada were both dismal. Many projects by major players had been stalled or stopped. Stories of companies going out of business were common, and getting money to start up a new marketing services firm—in Calgary!—was a laughable proposition. But my partners and I looked at the big picture and persuaded ourselves that these conditions were actually advantageous for building a new type of marketing firm, one that offered not just traditional creative services—advertising, essentially—but also strategy, media and PR. Our reasoning went like this: We're offering integrated marketing so companies will flock to us because we're the smart option. To us, it seemed like a no-brainer. It just took a few years for the marketplace to figure that out, too.

Even if you're not an entrepreneur, thinking like one can help you persuade yourself to try to move forward. You can train yourself to look for opportunity, instead of telling yourself you face impossible odds. You can persuade yourself to concentrate on potential, not problems. You can view setbacks as a challenge to dig deeper, not as proof that you don't have what it takes to succeed. You can take the view that your effort and attitude will in large part determine where you go—and, even more important, will determine how you feel about yourself while you're getting there.

THE STORY YOU TELL YOURSELF SHAPES YOUR LIFE

As events have proved, my main obstacle to success in the first three decades of my life wasn't a lack of intelligence or education or even opportunity. It was my own story about myself. There was nowhere to go in that story except down. Subsequently, I've worked very hard and had some very good luck, but the crucial ingredient of my success has been changing my narrative from one of self-criticism and failure to one of self-acceptance and possibility. I persuaded myself I had potential, not just problems. Otherwise, I would never have had the courage even to *try* to get somewhere in the business world.

Here's the thing: the tale I'd been telling myself about my life wasn't an objective catalogue of events and relationships, created after the fact. No one's story is. It's a subjective interpretation we construct to make sense of the past. We tell ourselves stories to try to figure out what's happened to us and what it all means—and those stories also *shape* events, in both subtle and obvious ways. Let's say your story about yourself is that you're a proud and beautiful woman oppressed by a controlling husband—well, you're going to view your life quite differently than you would if you told yourself you were a scatter-brained bimbo with the good luck to be married to a man who can take care of you. Both stories might correspond to the facts just about equally. But the one you choose to believe will have a huge impact on how you feel about yourself and what you do in the future. In the first case, you're going to feel resentful and might be headed for divorce court; in the second, you're going to feel grateful and try your damnedest to hang on to the guy.

Growing up, I learned first-hand how our stories about ourselves not only sum up our view of the past but also influence the future. My mother never wanted to leave South Africa, and in the early years, she hated living in Canada. The push-pull between my parents was something my sisters and I were always aware of, even as little girls. One of my clearest childhood memories—I would've been about seven years old—is of sitting in our old clunker of a car outside a dealership in Calgary. My parents had bought the car, used, when we came to Canada, and now it had broken down yet again. My dad was inside the dealership, negotiating, and my mother was sitting in the car, suffering silently. My sisters and I knew enough to know we'd better not act up.

Then my dad came back to the car. I remember what happened next as completely soundless, like a silent movie. He just stared at my mother, who had the only thing of value we could possibly trade for a car: her wedding ring, a perfect blue-white diamond that her father, a diamond cutter, had crafted especially for her. She was a beautiful woman, accustomed to male attention. To her, that ring wasn't just a connection to her family and to South Africa. It also symbolized the kind of life she felt she ought to have had, one with a lot more glamour. But she pulled it off her finger and gave it to my father. The ring was probably worth 20 times the value of the car my father traded it for. And that ring-for-car trade became part of our family's mythology.

But my parents' stories about the incident were completely different. For my father, it was a story about my mother's lack of pragmatism, wanting to hang on to that ring when clearly we needed a car. For my mother, it was a defining, highly emotional moment that summed up everything she'd had to sacrifice for her marriage. I understand, completely, why she felt that way. But in years to come, everything that happened between my parents was, in her book, just another chapter in that same sad story.

If the events had remained exactly the same but her narrative about them had changed—to one about how they'd pulled together during tough times, say, or about my father's poor negotiating skills—her life, both with my father and apart, might also have been very different.

CHANGING YOUR STORY

I didn't take stock in any objective way until things fell apart when I was 30. Up until that point, my story had been about my personality flaws and failings, my inferiority, my bad marriage. So I had two choices. I could conclude that this story was accurate—I really was a failure—and sink into a deep depression. Or I could conclude that my narrative had helped create the situation I found myself in and try to rewrite it. But there's just no place to go in a story where you cast yourself as a martyr or a victim or in some way not responsible for your own life. You're basically giving up on the possibility of taking the wheel and trying to steer your life in a direction you might actually want to go.

Given the nature of my marriage and the custody battle that followed, I could've viewed myself as the victim of a critical man, an unfair family law system, my church. But what would the point have been? It wouldn't have fixed anything or made me feel any better. And I certainly wouldn't have been in the right frame of mind to try to propel myself into a career if I'd focused on how wounded I felt. Nor would I have learned the lessons I needed to learn about taking responsibility for my own life. So instead I chose a story with the best chance of a happy ending, one where I was the author, shaping (and, yes, misshaping) the plot.

Divorce, even when the marriage has been miserable, is a huge shock to the system. It forces you to re-evaluate what you thought you knew about yourself and retrace the steps of your journey to try to figure out where you went wrong. Like most women, I didn't set out to make my mother's mistakes. Yet I did. I'd tried to be the perfect wife and mother, and wound up divorced. It gave me a lot of sympathy for my mom and helped me better understand her decisions. But I wanted my post-divorce life to go differently. And that meant accepting that I was accountable for everything prior to that point.

My dad was always very big on accountability. I remember the first time I drank alcohol as a teen. My father came into my room—it was instantly obvious I'd been drinking, my breath stank to high heaven—and said, "I know sometimes you'll make a bad choice, but I trust that you will *know* it's a bad choice and understand that you have to live with it. When you behave dishonestly, you have to ask yourself, Do I like who I am? Do I feel good about my choice?" He taught me that our choices define who we are. You **cannot**, later down the road, pin the blame for them on anyone else.

We talked about this a lot when I was staying with him after my divorce, and those conversations gave me a different perspective on my past. Looking back, I realized that my real problem wasn't a husband who I found overbearing; it was my own insecurity. I'd felt lucky that anyone wanted to marry me and also felt this might be my last chance—crazy thinking at any age, but especially at 19. I was so focused on feeling grateful that a man wanted to spend his life with me that I didn't stop to consider how I really felt about him and whether I was making a good choice. No one forced me to walk down the aisle. The exact opposite was true. My parents tried to persuade me not to get married. They told me, in the nicest possible way, that I wasn't mature enough to make such an important decision. And they were right, as parents usually are.

No one forced me to stay in my marriage, either. My narrative had been that I was trapped, with no way out, because a good Mormon wife never leaves. But, of course, I had options (ones that were a lot more dignified and ethical than having an affair). They were just options that involved risks I wasn't brave enough to take.

In retrospect, I can see clearly that even while I'd been busy telling myself I couldn't stand on my own two feet, I was developing managerial ability and a high tolerance for stress—I was working full-time, parenting four kids, and building a house, for goodness' sake! But I'd been so dedicated to my poor self-image, it was like wearing blinders that shielded me from seeing anything positive about myself.

So the most important mind I had to change was my own. Instead of constantly telling myself, "You can't do it, you're not smart enough," I started to tell myself, "It's a new challenge, I'll learn something." I also started to reframe my past. Instead of "My husband didn't love me because I'm unlovable," I opted for "I got married way too young." Instead of "I'm a horrible person who deserves to suffer because I had an affair," my understanding became "I did something wrong that I can't take back, and I've learned a really hard and painful lesson about values and the consequences of moral compromise."

I don't want to imply that I bucked up my spirits with some sunny platitudes and suddenly life was perfect. In fact, I think it's a terrible idea to tell yourself, "I'm a brilliant person who deserves success." Affirmations like that are meaningless, if not delusional, and also provide another way of ducking responsibility for moving forward. The truth is, the world doesn't owe any of us. We owe ourselves.

Which is why, especially if you feel stuck, it's a good idea to take a hard look at your own narrative. Think about how you'd tell your life story to a Hollywood producer, how you'd explain the highs and lows. Have you cast yourself as a victim of circumstance? If so, maybe your story could use a rewrite, starting with a lead character who has choices—and sometimes makes the wrong ones.

Rewriting my narrative changed my view of my present as well as my understanding of my prospects for the future. I didn't twist the facts. I just looked at them from a different angle. In my new story, the mistakes I'd made weren't tragedies. They were errors I learned from.

Successes weren't flukes. They were proof that I had some good qualities. This new story about myself helped me dry my tears, get up off my dad's couch, and try to do something constructive.

At some point, you have to decide just to get on with it, no matter how bad you feel about yourself or how afraid you are. It's one of those simple yet incredibly difficult things to do, like stepping off the high diving board. You just have to ignore your fear—and that voice in your head that's screaming, "You can't do this!"—and make yourself do it.

Quite frankly, poverty can be helpful in this regard—you have no choice but to get going if you want to eat. My father and his wife were emotionally supportive, but they were in no position to carry me financially. I *had* to figure out how to support myself and my kids. The more comfortable you are, the less urgency there is to change your situation. And the more time you have for second-guessing yourself and imagining every possible catastrophe, the harder it becomes to take action. You can wind up dithering on the sidelines of your own life, unsure what to do, while opportunity after opportunity slips past.

YOU CAN'T BASE YOUR LIFE'S DECISIONS ON POTENTIAL FUTURE REGRETS

Venture's president, Jen Cioffi, often makes a point to our clients that I just love. She tells them they have to be willing to put a stake in the ground—and then reserve the right to get smarter. What she means is that you have to start somewhere, even if it turns out not to be perfect. You can always adjust later on.

A lot of senior executives wallow in indecision, fearful of making a move that might turn out to be a mistake that could halt their career progression. In my experience, though, waffling does even more harm. Very frequently, it's the people who have the courage to be decisive, even if the outcome is less than optimal, who wind up with the corner office.

It's worth thinking about this if you feel stuck, either professionally or in some other way. After I give a speech, almost always a few members of the audience will approach me to ask for advice. These conversations often start like this: "I'm just not sure yet what I should do, career-wise. I don't want to make a choice I end up regretting." They're paralyzed by indecision; the issue isn't having too few choices but too many. Putting a stake in the ground is about attempting— saying, "I'm going to try, even if this turns out to be a mistake, in which case, I'll go to plan B." If you wait until you're 100 percent sure, you may miss the chance. And if you wait until success is guaranteed, you most definitely will be waiting forever.

To move forward, you need to persuade yourself to act, and to arm yourself against the consequences of your decision by deciding beforehand that it's all right to change your mind down the road, and also all right to make a mistake. Your decision doesn't need to be perfect. It just needs to be a decision. We all know dabblers who have never really found their path in life, often because they've been unwilling to commit with any level of seriousness to any single path for any length of time. They're too afraid they might regret closing other doors. My advice is to make the best decision you can for now, and continue to evaluate going forward, since you won't know until you're fairly immersed in a line of work or a way of life whether the fit is right.

Whenever I'm debating some course of action—whether Venture should bid for a piece of work, say, or whether I should offer a deal to a pitcher on *Dragons' Den*—I ask myself a series of pretty simple questions. Am I prepared to put up with the pain of a bad decision? If this turns out to be a mistake, can I learn from it? Can I still move forward? And always, most importantly, What's the worst thing that could happen? And then I force myself to act.

The first step can be the hardest one. It feels too important. Law school or Bay Street? You've been at the big corporation for years— should you stay or strike out on your own? When you can't decide, inertia sets in and you're open to being persuaded by someone else— your mother, your spouse, a colleague, a friend. It might feel safer to give up your vote than to own the consequences of the decision, for better or for worse. That way, later, if it turns out to have been a mistake, you can always tell yourself you're not to blame: you got bad advice, you were misled.

Now, I don't like making mistakes, and I don't like losing money. But I would rather do either than think of myself as not being in charge of my destiny. So I'm a little evangelical on this topic. You need to be in charge of your direction. Don't ever hand that over to someone else. You are much more likely to make the right choices for yourself much more often than someone else would. And in any case, your free agency is worth so much more than any potential repercussions you might experience from bad decisions.

If you own your choices, it's more likely you can persuade yourself to make changes and try to move forward. And if you're in charge of your own voice, it gives you so much more freedom. But people tend to think of it the other way around. They give up control because they don't want to make mistakes. But, in fact, mistakes are exactly what let you understand who you are and help you grow.

I learned the hard way how important it is to control your own narrative. As a 19-year-old Mormon, I belonged to a church that told me marriage is forever, no matter what. By the time I was 29, this had become part of my narrative and a compelling reason to stay in an unhappy marriage. My husband's views, too, had been incorporated into my internal monologue. I didn't just give up my own voice. I internalized what I heard as his: you're not attractive enough, not lovable enough, not capable enough.

This taught me a lesson that's served me well in business, which is that in the absence of your own narrative, someone will always supply it for you. And it's much easier to accept another person's narrative than to reject it and create your own. But unless physical coercion or psychological torture is involved, you can't blame anyone else for what you persuade yourself is true. And I do not blame him. If you've convinced yourself you can't do something, you are ultimately responsible for your belief—and you must take responsibility for persuading yourself you were wrong.

TALKING YOURSELF OUT OF TALKING YOURSELF OUT OF THINGS

When I'm trying to persuade myself of something, I don't pay attention to just my feelings. I also pay very close attention to my words and thoughts. Becoming aware of exactly what you're telling yourself, then rationally deconstructing the message, really helps short-circuit negative self-talk. For instance, as soon as the I-can't-do-it internal monologue starts, ask yourself, Why *can't* I ask for a raise/apply for a new job/go back to school/launch my own business? If you finish the thought and really try to explain your reasoning, almost always the explanation will involve a fear of some sort: you're afraid you're not talented enough, or not gregarious enough, or not a good enough manager, or too old, or too whatever. You're afraid you don't have what it takes and might fail—and might embarrass yourself.

Think of what you'd say to a friend who told you she couldn't do something because she just wasn't smart enough, or wasn't good with people, or wasn't creative enough. You would try to persuade her otherwise—not to be nice, but because you'd be able to see clearly that her fear wasn't entirely rational and that there were solutions to many of the problems she viewed as insurmountable obstacles. It's easier to be objective about someone else's situation, since negative emotion is removed from the equation; you don't feel whatever fear it is that's holding the other person back. So it's much less difficult to pitch a friend on her abilities and potential. You'd point out her proven strengths, including examples not just from her work life but also her personal life—"Remember when your boss asked you to make a presentation at that conference in Victoria? He must think you're competent or he wouldn't have asked. And what about the time you organized everyone in the neighbourhood to clean up the park?" As she continued to raise objections you'd counter them: "Okay, let's say you're right and you need retraining. What's stopping you from going back to school? Yes, it would be tough logistically, but you could do it." In other words, you'd be able to see clearly that the real issues were (a) a confidence gap that wasn't borne out by the facts, and (b) a negative pattern of thinking that wasn't realistic or productive.

This is exactly the kind of logical, concrete approach you need to take with yourself when your own negative self-talk tape loop has been activated. Talk to yourself the same way you'd talk to a friend, focusing on strengths and potential—what you *can* do, based on what you've done in the past—rather than weaknesses and problems. Of course, you need to be realistic and practical, just as you would with a friend. If you've been unemployed for a year and have exhausted every avenue you can think of to find a job in your field, there's no point in pretending to yourself that there's a pot of gold right around the corner. But there's also no point in telling yourself, "I'm a loser, that's why no one wants to hire me." You need to think concretely about your situation in order to make it more manageable: "I'm unable to find a job at this moment in time, partly because of the economy and changes in my field. I'm going to have to look at doing something new." Mistakes and setbacks aren't the end of the world. Whether you view them as catastrophes or, alternatively, as learning opportunities will in large part determine whether you're able to bounce back and land somewhere you want to be.

When you're trying to persuade yourself to do something, look realistically at the worst-case scenario. Okay, maybe you try something and you fail. What's the downside? Well, maybe you'll feel bad about yourself, and maybe you'll feel embarrassed—what if people view you differently, knowing you failed? This reasoning doesn't really stand up to scrutiny. People who are close to us don't generally judge us by or even care about our professional failures (or successes, for that matter). And if they do, so what? Ultimately, it's your life, and you only get one shot. So you also need to consider the downside if you don't attempt something that feels scary or risky. What potential gains would you miss out on? What's the impact on your life today and on your future?

Try using some of the same tactics you use when persuading yourself you *can't* do something. Be just as creative and resourceful: "I'd love to work outside the home, and both kids are at school full time now, so I can focus on finding a job. Once I'm making some money, I'll be able to hire a sitter to help after school. I may have to retrain or take a course—hey, that could turn out to be a good way to network. And being home with the kids for a few years has helped me develop some strengths that will really benefit me in any job. I'm a much better multi-tasker now, more patient, and more interested in learning new things and stretching myself intellectually. Finding a new job won't be easy, but if I met the challenge of motherhood, I can do this, too."

Play devil's advocate, but this time, argue for the defence rather than the prosecution. For instance, years ago when I was trying to decide whether I should join Venture, I debated both sides of the question in my head, converting liabilities into assets. There was no guaranteed income—but I'd have a stake in the company. I didn't have a degree or much relevant experience—so I wasn't bound by traditional ways of thinking. I wasn't polished—but I was genuine, and clients liked that. I'd flown under the radar, a passive observer—so I'd watched closely and learned what makes people tick, which is key in marketing. I didn't really know what marketing was all about—this would be a great learning opportunity. I might fail—I could always bail if it didn't work out.

My narrative could have been that my past made a future at Venture impossible—I just didn't have the right stuff. Or the story could be that my past—all the trials and tribulations of growing up, fending for myself so young and learning how to make jam and be creative with macaroni dinners—contained really useful lessons that could be applied in business.

Ever since I was little, I've talked to myself. To this day, I remember what I said to persuade myself to join Venture: "You were scared when you started at the TV station and when you got divorced, too. But you survived. You pick new things up quickly—isn't that what you just did at the TV station? And before that, learning to grow cucumbers and make pickles?"

And then I asked myself one more question I have subsequently asked at every career crossroads. What have you got to lose? If the answer is "Well, you could lose face," my reaction, after spending 31 years of my life paralyzed by fear of failure and embarrassment, is always the same. I hold my breath and jump. And if that's the only thing holding you back, you should, too.

CHAPTER SIX

"I'm not good enough"

One day in 2007, the phone rang in my Toronto office. "Hi, it's Mike Armitage over at the CBC. I work on *Dragons' Den*—have you heard of the show?"

"Yes," I said. In fact, I watched it regularly and was a bit of an armchair dragon. "You must be looking for a media director, let me transfer you to—"

"No," he replied, "I'm not. I'm wondering if you'd like to audition to be a female dragon." It was so out of left field, I thought it was a practical joke. When he convinced me he wasn't kidding and asked to meet me, my main thought was "No one is going to believe this." I was intrigued—this had all the makings of a great story—but didn't take the conversation seriously. Me on TV? Ridiculous.

A few days later, three of the show's producers came to my office. Now, I spend a lot of time in meetings, but I'd never had one like this before. You know when someone is really staring at you, and you begin to worry that you have a piece of spinach or something stuck in your teeth? Well, it was just like that, times three. The questions they were asking, too, weren't ones I was used to hearing in my board-room: "How do you feel about dealing with aggressive men? Are you married? Your children, what are they like?"

It was like being under a microscope, even before they got to the really important questions. "Have you ever done any investing?" Yes, I'd done some angel investing, loans to help entrepreneurs get their businesses off the ground, but strictly small-time stuff. "Ever been on camera before?" Twenty years ago, during my short-lived stint at the Calgary TV station, I'd been in a few commercials—one for a land company, another for a radio station—along with co-workers when the station needed cheap talent. But since then, nothing. The produc-ers also wanted to know about Venture, about Calgary, about my past. The whole experience was a bit disorienting, and I went home unsure whether I should audition or not. Did I really want to open myself up to even more scrutiny? And what if, after laying my life bare, I was rejected?

My kids listened to all this, not very patiently, and then said, "Are you crazy? You *have* to do it. Like you're always saying, what's the worst that could happen?" It was one of those classic parenting moments, when your own words, delivered with a little too much glee, come back to haunt you.

The worst that could happen? The producers would decide they'd made a terrible mistake asking me to try out. They'd figure out I just wasn't good enough to be on the show. Now my kids really weren't patient. "So what? Then you won't get the job. But maybe you won't want it, either."

They were right. Auditioning wasn't the same as being asked to appear on the show. I decided the best attitude to take was "what the hell, this is just a lark." So a couple of days later, I walked into the lobby of the CBC building in Toronto and immediately bumped into

Kevin O'Leary, who was being fussed over like a bit of a celebrity. Still unclear about what was going to happen next, I went into the makeup room with him and three other women who were also auditioning. The atmosphere, all bustle then strange pockets of silence, felt weirdly familiar, as I'd been on set many times when Venture produced commercials for our clients.

Before we walked onto the stage, there was no prep or coaching. We sat down—I was placed beside Kevin, in the same chair where I now sit on the show—and the first pitch started. I was aware of the cameras but tried to view the situation just like any other meeting: you have to listen very closely to the pitch and be unafraid to jump in with questions. I didn't feel uncomfortable, as I'd expected to, as this was all about my professional expertise, not about me as a person, and I had years of experience to draw on. Kevin was doing his thing, I was jumping in, and I kept trying to create space for the other women to speak up, but they didn't. That was my main concern, actually, that they weren't talking enough and we were talking too much.

When the audition was over I unclipped my microphone, thinking, "That was interesting and fun," and went back to the office knowing I'd never hear from the producers again. Being in the CBC building with all those big blown-up posters of TV celebrities had confirmed for me that I wasn't meant to be one of them. I didn't look a thing like them, and besides, I already had a pretty good job.

So I was extremely surprised, to put it mildly, to be called back for a second audition. And this time, I thought long and hard beforehand about whether I actually wanted the job. I didn't like the idea of losing my privacy, but on the other hand, at that point, *Dragons' Den* had only 200,000 viewers. It wasn't as though I'd be mobbed by autograph seekers every time I set foot outside my house. And there was a lot that appealed to me about the show itself. I thought the concept was very smart, and I liked the idea of making entrepreneurship sexy and helping people realize their dreams. The set-up was realistic in that it mirrored what I see all the time in my business: people don't understand that you can have the best idea in the world, but if you don't know how to take it to the marketplace, it won't be successful.

My thinking went like this: This is a great opportunity to have a new experience, and the downside is relatively minor—I'll still have Venture, after all. Yes, I might make a fool of myself, but so what? Not that many people watch the show anyway. Maybe, if I got the role, I'd be on the show for only a year. Certainly I wouldn't have to sign on for life.

So yes, I decided, I did want to be a dragon (how's that for a job title?), which meant I really had to go for it in the second audition. Yet some part of me was still hesitant. And the main thing holding me back, the source of my reluctance, was a fear of not being good enough.

CONVERT A SENSE OF INFERIORITY TO FUEL THAT HELPS YOU MOVE FORWARD

I am pretty confident of my skills in business, but thinking about doing something different, like a TV show, brought back some of the insecurities I'd had when I was first starting out. What if I wasn't as good as everyone else? What if I couldn't hold my own against the other entrepreneurs on the show? What if I didn't measure up when it came to making deals?

On an intellectual level, I know perfectly well that formidable competition shouldn't be an incentive to pack it in and head for home—it should be an incentive to try to take your game up a notch and see what you're made of. On an emotional level, however, the feeling of inferiority still resonates and can make me feel small and uncertain when I'm trying to do something new. It takes me right back to high school, where I coped with it by flying under the radar and turning away from challenges and opportunities. I have a different coping mechanism now, obviously, but I wish I could simply banish the feeling of being less-than—as you might be able to do if you're lucky.

If you're more like me, however, you'll have to defuse the feeling of relative inadequacy by using it as an impetus to compete. Sometimes it's enough simply to take a step back and imagine how you'd react if someone said, "You're just not good enough, you'll never measure up to other people." Very likely you'd be insulted, and hell-bent on proving the other person wrong.

Certainly, that's true in my case. I'd be offended if anyone else said half the things to me that I sometimes say to myself. And I'd channel that anger to drive my performance. That's what I've always done when others have been skeptical of my abilities—I've used their skepticism as fuel to help me drive forward. My response has been, *I'll show you.* For instance, about six years ago, Venture was doing more and more work in Toronto, so I decided to open an office in the city. There was some eye rolling in Calgary; no other independent firm had successfully branched out in Toronto, with its plethora of agencies. Who did we think we were, trying to play with the big boys? And in Toronto, there was a sense that, being from Calgary, we were bush league. (This was back in the day when Toronto was the centre of the universe, before western Canada came to be seen as a formidable economic powerhouse.) The skeptics made me only more determined to succeed. Even if they'd been right and Venture had crashed and burned in Toronto, I know I'd rather have tried to succeed than spend the rest of my life wondering, "What if?"

I've failed enough times to know this about myself for sure: I find it much easier to live with failure than to live with regret over the road not taken.

So when I'm the person telling myself I just can't measure up, I try to view the situation exactly the same way I would if someone else expressed doubt about my capabilities, as a challenge to prove myself.

TRY TO VIEW YOUR DIFFERENCES AS ASSETS, NOT LIABILITIES

Another practical approach is to look at the situation from another perspective. Okay, so you're *not* the same as other people in the organization or field. But differences aren't necessarily weaknesses. They can also be strengths. Instead of persuading yourself you lack the right qualifications, ask yourself, What do I have to offer that's unique? And answer this question in the same spirit you would if a friend asked it: generously but realistically, focusing on the upside.

Before my second *Dragons' Den* audition, for instance, when I was worrying about whether I deserved a place at the table, I stopped and asked myself what I could bring to the table. What was missing that I might be able to supply? Thinking about the situation this way helped me to frame my differences as assets instead of liabilities. No, I wasn't as flashy a mogul as some of the dragons—and that was probably a plus, that my style and approach are down-to-earth and closer to the average Canadian's. No, my business isn't worth billions—but through Venture, I've touched more industries and businesses at the strategic level than the other dragons have, so I have a broader knowledge base. And no, I don't think like a banker, solely in terms of dollars and cents—I think more about how to get an idea to market. The other dragons' businesses are very specific to a particular industry, and they approach every pitch from the perspective of owning and managing a business; I approach every pitch from the perspective of what the market wants. We just don't see business through the same lens. Realizing this, I also realized that being different might well be exactly what qualified me to be on the show.

THE 15 MINUTES OF FAME THEORY

One way to persuade yourself to take risks that might end in failure is to focus not just on what you'll learn along the way but also on the fact that, win or lose, this gamble isn't going to be what defines you. Unless you let it. I call this the 15 minutes of fame theory. Maybe you'll get to centre stage only to fall flat on your face, but the spotlight will move on, and whatever happened while it was shining on you will not be the sum total of your life and experience. In fact, chances are good that everyone else will forget all about your performance, even if it was brilliant.

This idea, that whatever you're doing that feels so earth-shaking and significant at the moment is probably just a blip in the larger picture of your life, can be really calming, especially when you're worried about embarrassing yourself. In a high-stakes pitch situation where keeping a sense of perspective can be challenging, it helps to take the attitude, "So what if I make a fool of myself? No one else will even remember a year from now." So before my second audition for the show, when I'd decided I did want to be a dragon, instead of psyching myself out, I told myself, "This is really no big deal to anyone else, it's just my 15 minutes." (I read somewhere that some professional athletes do something similar before a big competition, telling themselves it doesn't really matter, that it's just a game.)

115

Then I approached the audition exactly the same way I've been advising you to pitch. I prepared beforehand by watching the show and thinking about what the producers wanted and needed, what they might feel was missing from the show. And when taping began, I conducted myself exactly as I would in any persuasion situation. I kept my mouth shut, resisted the urge to show off or prove what I know, and gave each pitcher my undivided attention. The questions I asked were mostly around subtext: "Why did you come up with this business idea, what was driving you?" And when it came time to offer an opinion, I spoke from the heart, kept it simple, made sure I was heard, and stayed focused on the pitcher rather than the cameras.

I got the job, as you know. And then came the hard part: I had to deliver. I'm still working on that . . .

DON'T COMPARE YOUR INTERIOR TO ANYONE ELSE'S EXTERIOR

Unless you're one of those rare people who was born feeling you could handle whatever life throws your way, self-confidence may not be easy to summon. Many people who appear clearly competent, gifted even, just don't have a lot of faith in themselves. I think one reason is that they compare how they feel inside with the way high achievers appear on the outside—confident, accomplished, competent—and wind up feeling inferior. Needlessly.

The fact that someone has been elevated in some way doesn't necessarily mean he feels any different inside than you do. In case you've missed it, I have exactly the same insecurities anyone else has. If anything, they're even more overwhelming when you know a couple of million people are seeing all your flaws in high definition!

Yet the myth persists that business leaders and people with a public profile have some kind of special armour that protects against uncertainty and self-doubt. It's funny to me, given how many of them I know, that anyone thinks senior executives and other high achievers don't have the same hang-ups, issues, and weaknesses as everyone else. Some of them have even more. Certainly, the most insecure people I've ever met have been either famous or extremely accomplished in their fields. Some seem to require almost constant approval just to get through the day. They believe their own press—yet doubt it, too, which is why they need applause the way the rest of us need oxygen.

So I've learned not to take my measure as a professional or as a person by comparing myself with the way others appear on the outside. Other people's externals rarely match the internals, so why waste your time jumping at shadows? Frankly, why compare yourself to someone else at all? Constantly looking over your shoulder gives you a very skewed perspective on the world. We *all* have strengths and weaknesses, and plenty of room for self-improvement. But it should be driven by self-awareness, not hyper-consciousness of others. If you measure your worth against other people's accomplishments, you'll only turn up the volume on your inner critic and wind up feeling even worse about yourself.

Here's something else I know: fear of not being good enough and not measuring up to other people is one of the best excuses there is to not bother trying. What starts as an explanation for reluctance to take risks can harden into a full-blown excuse for inertia. Frankly, if you truly believe you're not good enough, the last thing you should do is sit back. You should focus on doing whatever you can to get strong enough to take the next step, whether that means going back to school, or learning a new language, or looking for a new job, or trying to change fields, or seeking coaching, or whatever it will take.

YOUR MEASURES OF SUCCESS
DETERMINE HOW SUCCESSFUL YOU FEEL

As you go further up in the stratosphere of the business world, you don't encounter a whole lot of humility. The older I get, the stranger that seems. If you're honest with yourself, you know that your achievements are pretty inconsequential in the grand scheme of things. So you started a company, it did well, and you wound up with money. It's not nothing, but . . . so what? There are always going to be people out there who built something even bigger and better—as well as people who did something truly heroic, or something that benefited humankind, or something that dazzled and entertained the world.

This is one big problem with measuring success quantitatively, by which I mean in terms of how much money you make or how many rungs of the ladder you climb. You may *never* actually feel successful, even if you reach or surpass your goals, because there will always be someone who has more and who went further. And frankly, I just don't think it's possible to fill an emotional void with money or degrees or titles.

It seems to me that the real questions to ask yourself are these: Did you hold on to your values and conduct yourself honourably? Did you make the world a slightly better place? Did you enjoy the journey? Did you acquire the wisdom of humility? If from the beginning those are your measures of achievement, you'll be far better armed to ignore negative self-talk and to avoid the trap of comparing yourself with others. And you'll probably feel a lot more confident because even if you've never held a job, you already have a good idea from your behaviour toward others in everyday situations whether you're capable of living up to your own ethical standards. Instead of feeling not good enough, you're likely to feel pretty good about your chances of success.

And there's another, perhaps even more important, reason to use ethical measures to gauge your achievement. You'll likely be far more fulfilled by what you actually do manage to accomplish if you assess your performance relative to your own values, instead of comparing your outcome with someone else's. You're levelling the playing field, in a sense. It won't be possible for someone to wind up with more than you, and you won't feel that someone else's success takes away from yours. Your main competitor will be yourself, running on a course you designed.

Who you are—your values, your core beliefs, and how you implement them in the business world—is a much more satisfying measure of self-worth than how much money you make or where you stand on the corporate ladder. And it's also the only measure that will make you feel good enough to try your hand at just about anything.

THE OBSTACLES IN YOUR PATH

Most people have a natural talent for persuasion. The problem for many is that they wield it against themselves and convince themselves either that they don't deserve success or that it's unattainable for reasons beyond their control. But self-persuasion doesn't need to be destructive. It can, with some effort, be converted to a constructive tool that helps you change your narrative from one of limitation to one of possibility. The key is to train yourself to think like an entrepreneur, one who sees potential even in problems, and to talk to yourself the same way you would talk to a friend: logically and encouragingly, with plenty of concrete examples.

Another thing that helps is bearing in mind that just about everyone, even people who on the surface seem to be incredibly accomplished and self-assured, struggles with self-doubt and feelings of inferiority. Emotionally, anyway, the playing field is actually more level than it appears. You can level it further depending on how you choose to define success for yourself. If your measures of achievement revolve around your principles rather than tangible outcomes, it will be easier to feel successful—and easier to persuade yourself that you have what it takes to go even further.

PART FOUR

THE PROCESS OF PERSUASION

Persuasion is part of so many high-stakes situations. You need to be good at it when you're asking for a loan, lobbying for a raise, negotiating a sensitive issue with siblings, trying to land a seat on the board or attract a new client—and when you're trying to persuade yourself to take a risk and follow your dreams. But if you're like most people, you may have no clue how to go about it, much less how to adjust your approach to suit different situations. The last time you probably thought in any depth about the process of persuasion was in grade seven or eight, when you had to write an essay arguing for some political policy—and another essay arguing against it.

Most people have never been taught the mechanics of real-life persuasion and tend to think it's all about content: if your argument is strong enough, it will speak for itself. Well, it's true that you need a well-crafted pitch to move people from "no" or "maybe" to "yes." *But at least half of what makes you persuasive occurs before you ever even open your mouth.* Before you utter a word, you need to prepare, you need to rein in your ego, and you need to figure out what's driving the other party. How well you do those three things will, in many cases, largely determine how persuasive you are. But because persuasion is an interaction, success depends not just on you but also on the other party. You need to understand the people you're persuading. What's motivating them? What do they want? How do they view the situation?

To persuade others that what you're suggesting is in their best interests, not just yours, you must be able to answer those questions. It's astonishing how often people go into critically important meetings armed with spreadsheets, an impressive track record, and lofty-sounding mission statements and promises, yet with no clue what the other party actually wants. And it's amazing how many people approach negotiations with people they know quite well—friends, colleagues, neighbours—without really thinking about their needs.

That's what Part IV is all about: figuring out what other people want and need, and how to craft a compelling message that speaks directly to them.

CHAPTER SEVEN

Prepare

So, how *do* you persuade other people? Although there's no formula that will work every time, it's helpful to think about persuasion as a process with distinct but overlapping stages. At first this might seem counterintuitive—a really good persuader makes it look so easy. Effortless, even. People occasionally speak of being lulled into agreement without even recognizing at the time that they were being persuaded.

In reality, however, persuading someone usually requires considerable effort, starting with careful preparation. You need to do your homework, particularly if the other person already has a strong opinion and/or you have a limited amount of time to make your case. What line of reasoning is most likely to appeal? What should you definitely not say? And to maximize your chances of success, you need to be well versed in the pros and cons of whatever you're proposing, you need to anticipate objections and be able to come up with potential solutions, and you must know your material and line of argument so well that you can speak fluently. Confidently, too. If you yourself don't sound persuaded of your idea, it's going to be hard to talk anyone else into it.

Blindingly obvious? Not to a large number of business people. (It never fails to amaze me how many executives wing it in the boardroom, even when the stakes are high.) Nor to a large number of the hopeful entrepreneurs who appear on *Dragons' Den,* even though many of them have a lot riding on the outcome, both emotionally and financially. Most contestants on the show have invested their own— and sometimes their friends' and families'—savings in their business ideas. Often they're seeking backing not only because they want to take their business to another level but because, without help, they could lose everything they've invested.

Appearing on national television to pitch to potential investors is either their last best hope or the opportunity of a lifetime, and you'd think for that reason they'd be extraordinarily well prepared. But if you've watched the show, you know that isn't always the case. While many contestants arrive on the set with carefully assembled props and elaborate gimmicks, few have taken the time to anticipate the kinds of questions we'll ask or to gather the facts necessary to respond persuasively.

In situations where the stakes are lower—trying to convince the neighbours to help pay for the repair of a broken fence, say—people sometimes don't stop to prepare because they think they're just having a conversation, not trying to engage in persuasion. But even in low-key situations, figuring out beforehand what the other party needs and how to get there will make you more effective and more likely to get what you want.

In this chapter we'll look at how and why to lay the groundwork for a pitch, and also focus on the difference between preparation and presentation. I'll show you how good preparation provides armour against the unexpected and allows you to be flexible enough to respond to curve balls.

GETTING READY IS NOT THE FUN PART—IT'S THE ESSENTIAL PART

There's an old saying that the will to *prepare* is more important than the will to win, and I believe that's true. Most people want to win, and some even seem to feel entitled to instant success. But a surprisingly small number are willing to put in the effort.

Preparation is not fun. It's the long, hard slog toward success. It's difficult, gruelling even, and often both frustrating and a little boring. I remember having 90- and 100-hour work weeks in the early years of Venture, photocopying and binding presentations when I was so tired I could barely keep my eyes open. There was no glory in it. But if you're not willing to prepare, you'll never be ready to seize all the opportunities that come your way, since the best ones will require hard work.

People who have lasting success are almost always hard workers who approach each new challenge as though they're gearing up for their first big break. Being competitive by nature can help a lot. So can humility. Don't let yourself get cocky; it's simply not possible to coast on a degree from a prestigious university, or to rest on your laurels or your numbers from last year. The day you do that, you're finished—there are always hungry people lined up behind you, just waiting for a chance to take your place.

Knowing that I'm replaceable has really helped me stay grounded about being on a TV show. I wasn't on *Dragons' Den* in the first season; I was hired in the second season to replace one of the original dragons, so right from the start I've always been aware that I, too, could be traded in for a different model. In a heartbeat. In fact, the producers never stop auditioning new dragons, in case one of us gets hit by a bus, or wants off the show, or is seen to be a drag on the ticket. It's pretty hard to think of yourself as God's gift to television when you know your replacement is waiting in the wings. And it's a very good incentive to stay focused and work hard.

ENTHUSIASM AND PASSION AREN'T ENOUGH

Getting ready to persuade others requires systematically thinking through potential obstacles and possible objections, then coming up with solutions—or at least the right questions you should be asking. You need to have considered the flaws in your design so you can counter arguments effectively when others don't think your ideas are quite as brilliant as you do. Logic is a necessary and effective safety check on passion.

Enthusiasm is important, but it's not enough to make you persuasive. This is so clear on *Dragons' Den,* where most contestants tend to have exactly the same passion and risk tolerance as top entrepreneurs. But a lot of them haven't done the most elementary form of preparation: thinking through the basics of translating their bright idea into a profitable business. To me, this boils down to two very straightforward building blocks. First, every entrepreneur must have a value proposition; there has to be something unique about the product or service, and proof that the market needs it. And second, entrepreneurs need to come up with a business model that takes into account both the drivers of profit and the players necessary to make the business work; you have to know how to get your product to the consumer, whether there are health and safety regulations to be considered, what distribution networks already exist, and so on. (Similarly, in every situation involving persuasion, you need to understand the technical necessities and practical issues involved in whatever you're lobbying for, as well as the real merits of your idea. Say, for instance, you want your MP to champion a new bylaw. Part of preparation is coming up with a value proposition based on what you know the new law could accomplish—and the other part is figuring out what it is you don't yet know.)

But again and again, some people come on the show without having figured any of this out. And they seem to think that we won't do our homework, either. Not uncommonly, entrepreneurs proudly announce that their companies' valuation is a million dollars or more—though sales are minuscule or non-existent. They're not lying. That's really what they think their companies are worth. But often they can't answer basic questions like "*Why* do you think your company is worth a million dollars?" They've talked themselves into believing they're on the brink of huge success, yet many have no clue how to build or run a business, much less convince anyone else they can do these things. They're under the impression that bullshit baffles brains.

The entrepreneurs who do persuade us to give them money all share two attributes. They're well prepared and know what they're talking about, and they're also prepared to admit when they *don't* know something. In any pitch situation, whether it's on TV or over a table at the doughnut shop, you want to be confident that you know your material but not so full of yourself that you think you know everything. And you want to have practised beforehand so that you don't crumble under the stress of the situation. Many contestants who do get deals on the show say afterward how glad they are that they spent so much time getting ready, since the minute they got in front of the cameras, their brains froze. It was only because they'd practised and practised beforehand that they were able to get the words out. The drama of the situation and the heightened experience of pitching your idea in front of a dozen cameras, five pretty tough judges, and two million viewers is nerve-wracking. The people who cope best are those who've done their legwork so they can perform under stress.

This is true any time you have an emotional investment in a pitch and the stakes feel high, whether you're trying to persuade someone to give you money or a promotion or another chance. Your emotions can create exactly the same kind of stress that TV cameras do, which is why preparation is so important.

IT'S ALL RIGHT TO BE A LITTLE NERVOUS

Research shows that a bit of stress increases efficiency and improves performance. A touch of anxiety actually makes you a little sharper, a little more alert. Of course, there's a threshold; too much stress has the opposite effect. But my point is that nerves are not necessarily a bad thing when you're pitching, and they're certainly not a deal breaker—not on TV and not in real life, either.

Even the most confident public speakers have butterflies once in a while. Including me. Growing up in the Mormon church, you're encouraged to give short speeches on a regular basis, so I got used to public speaking early in life. It usually doesn't feel scary to me. However, the first time I was asked to chair an industry event attended by the greats and near-greats in marketing, I was so nervous that when I stood up to welcome everyone, my voice went up a register and cracked a few times. I hadn't even realized how intimidated I felt until I opened my mouth and out came those squeaks. I was mortified. But when I sat back down, Venture's creative director leaned over and whispered to me, "Don't worry, it was actually kind of endearing."

And that's how I think about it now, too, when I see that someone is nervous. Usually, it convinces me the person is genuine. Although a lot of experts say you should never acknowledge feeling nervous, I disagree. I don't think you should kick off a pitch with, "Look, I'm really nervous," as that sets an expectation of weakness. But if, after starting a presentation or interview, you find you're not expressing yourself clearly or solidly, it's fine to stop and say something like "You know, I guess I'm more nervous than I thought I was going to be."

Then you have to demonstrate that you can get past your nerves and be strong (which is, in fact, especially impressive if you started out wobbly). In other words, it's fine to show a little vulnerability so long as you can also be clear about your strength. There's never anything wrong with authenticity, in my opinion.

KNOW YOUR AUDIENCE

Preparing for persuasion is only partially about figuring out what you want and what you have to offer. *It's primarily about trying to figure out what matters—or what should matter—to the other party.* In marketing, Venture is often asked to bid on new business, and we know going into these types of meetings that we're up against other good firms that will pull out all the stops to try to dazzle the client and land the account.

As much as possible, I try to get our team to focus not on the other contenders and what they might say or do but on the client's actual business. We survey the marketplace, figuring out what the client's competitors are doing well (and not so well); we look at historical trends; we look for possible niches and opportunities for the client; we keep an eye out for obstacles and looming problems; we try to find out as much as possible about the client's corporate culture and the leaders' personalities. We try to immerse ourselves in their world and learn to speak their language in an attempt to understand what motivates and drives them. Gearing up for a single meeting can take a team of people weeks of research.

The main purpose of all this, though, is not to blow the client away with our brilliant insights into their industry. It's to ensure that we know the lay of the land well enough that during the meeting, we can look outward and focus on the client and the client's input, rather than looking inward and racking our brains for facts, figures, and something smart to say. When we know our material inside out, we can give the client our full attention. As with job interviews, or even dates, you have only a matter of minutes to persuade people you're genuine and to try to spark some sort of emotional connection. The better prepared you are, the more you can focus on keeping the other person engaged.

In a one-on-one meeting with someone you already know, such as your manager, or the principal of your child's school, or a client you've worked with before, part of preparing is considering how that person prefers to get information. Some people want all the minutia. Others prefer broad strokes. We adapt instinctively with people we know well: your friend may simply want to know whether you won or lost the tennis game, whereas your husband may be interested in a blow-by-blow breakdown. If you're pitching to someone and you're not sure how she likes to get information, consider how that person expresses herself. As a big thinker? Having a sharp eye for detail? Focused on strategy? Or on the bottom line? And ask someone who really knows her—an executive assistant is always a great source.

A brief note on cross-cultural differences, which could no doubt fill several volumes: if you're meeting with people whose culture is different from yours, try to find out beforehand how these differences might affect your pitch. In some cultures, for instance, "Maybe, let me think about it" really means "No way in hell." And on several occasions in my career, I've belatedly figured out from the deference being paid to the men in the room that it was culturally unacceptable for me, as a woman, to lead the pitch. This would've been useful information to have had beforehand, as I could've saved myself the bother of showing up.

PRESENTATION IS NOT THE SAME AS PREPARATION

Today, just about anyone with a computer can create sophisticated graphics and a professional-quality presentation with all the bells and whistles. Similarly, the democratization of fashion, with widely available inexpensive knock-offs of high-end clothing and endless web-based resources offering pointers from image consultants, means that just about anyone can put together a stylish ensemble.

Perhaps because sizzle and style are now easier to pull off, there's a greater cultural emphasis on packaging than ever before. And one unfortunate result is that many people put too much emphasis on presentation at the expense of content and, increasingly, even confuse presentation with preparation. In my experience, many people in audition situations worry far too much about slickness and far too little about substance.

This is particularly problematic for women, as we're conditioned to care so much about approval and to worry so much about how we measure up in terms of external packaging. And understandably so, since there's still a double standard in the business world.

Unfortunately, there's still a sentiment out there that how a woman looks is as important as what she thinks, says, or brings to the table. Even more unfortunately, women are sometimes the ones who feel this way. Because Venture works closely with a broad range of companies, I've been inside a lot of offices in a lot of different industries all over Canada. And not infrequently I see women dressed as though they're heading out to a nightclub and I have to restrain myself from asking, "You got up this morning thinking what, exactly?" It's clear that they're looking to be valued sexually rather than intellectually.

Now, I have no problem with wearing ruffles and looking feminine (which is not the same as wanting to look sexy). And I also think that if looking feminine opens a door, so be it. (Athletic men, after all, use their masculinity as a business asset all the time.) But after that, you'd better have something else of value to offer or you won't get very far. And as you get older, it will be harder and harder to maintain the value of your currency. Never forget that you are in business for the long haul and that, unlike the rest of life, where a woman can start to feel invisible as she gets older, your opportunities in the workplace may well improve with age. At 54, I feel the sky's the limit in terms of what I might still achieve in business. I very much doubt I'd feel this way if I'd spent my career focused on how I looked rather than concentrating on what I could bring to the table in terms of knowledge, skills, expertise, and judgment.

Ultimately, hyper-focusing on your appearance can be crippling to your sense of professional competence, especially if you're already unsure of your abilities. Worrying about how you look, what you're wearing, and whether other people find you attractive is a major distraction from what should be your real focus: your work and, in this case, your pitch.

And the more revealing and provocative your clothing is, the more it can interfere with your performance. This has been a pet theory of mine for years, and I recently discovered there's actually some scientific research to back it up. In one university experiment, female students were asked to do math problems—alone, in a change room, where no one else could see them—once wearing a sweater, and once wearing a bathing suit. Although the math problems were identical in terms of difficulty, the women scored significantly lower when wearing bathing suits. Male students' scores, however, weren't affected in the slightest by what they were wearing. They did equally well in the sweater and the bathing suit. Their clothing had no effect on their problem-solving ability, which isn't surprising given that men have never been told that their primary value is their decorative appeal. But women have, and occasionally still are, which is why, if you're female and serious about career advancement, you need to think about the messages you're sending not just to others but to yourself if you dress provocatively at work.

This isn't to say that men have no worries at all about their physical appearance. Many short men are acutely conscious of their height (and, by the way, studies also show a strong correlation between a man's height and his earnings). Men can also be very concerned about their hair or lack thereof—just look at Donald Trump's comb-over.

But fretting about how you look—or how slick your graphics are—is a waste of time that would be better spent actually preparing, researching, and finding out everything you can about the new job, the new piece of business, or whatever it is that you're trying to persuade someone to give you. Of course, your materials should be organized and you should be reasonably well groomed by the standards of your industry. But your ability to be persuasive depends much more on your willingness to do the heavy lifting of preparation: research, figuring out what you have to offer, and trying to find out what the other party wants and needs. Being tall, or wearing Prada, will get you only so far.

In fact, as I learned shortly after joining Venture, it's possible (though, granted, not advisable) to be persuasive even when you resemble a wet poodle.

PREPARATION IS YOUR ARMOUR WHEN
THE UNEXPECTED HAPPENS (AND IT WILL HAPPEN)

When I worked at the TV station in Calgary, I had a client who we'll call Steve who owned a company that sold hair care products. Steve was tall, handsome, impeccably put together, and looked like he'd just stepped off the cover of *GQ*. After I left the TV station and joined Venture, he called and said he wanted to get hairdressers across the country to participate in a co-op advertising program. (A commercial or print ad for a major product that also features the names of local stores is co-op advertising.) The big company, in this case Steve's, showcases its products and splits the cost of the ad with smaller retail outlets that otherwise couldn't afford that kind of campaign. Steve's idea was that Venture would go to Vancouver to pitch to 1,200 hairdressers when they gathered there for a conference at the Pan Pacific hotel and try to persuade them to hire us to execute his co-op advertising idea.

Venture was still in its infancy at this point. We didn't have a roster of clients, much less a steady stream of income. Mostly what we had were bills and—rather irrationally given the economic climate at that time—optimism.

This was the breakthrough we'd been waiting for: somebody was going to take a chance on us. I hung up the phone, ran down the hall calling out to my partners, high-fived—and mind you, this was just a chance to *pitch*, not a signed business deal. After a minute or two of dancing around and congratulating each other, we stopped and looked at one another. "Oh my God, how can we afford the airfare to Vancouver?" someone said. We were making virtually no money at that point.

But we decided we couldn't pass up this opportunity. We'd just have to figure out a way to do the trip on a shoestring. Fortunately, one partner had Air Miles, so we used points to get to Vancouver. Another partner had a friend who said we could stay on his boat instead of at a hotel, to save money. I'd never sailed before in my life, and when we arrived at Maple Bay, off Vancouver Island, I noticed the boat's name was *Important Business*. I suddenly realized what my partners meant when they'd told me in the past that they were "going away on important business." They were talking about this sailboat. I would've been mad, except that now I got to join them. I really felt I'd arrived.

We sailed away and as we got closer to Vancouver, someone asked, "Can we anchor offshore, so we don't have to pay for a slip in the harbour?" I shrugged and said, "Sure." I didn't know anything about it, what did I care? We stayed up all night working on our presentation—writing, rewriting, tweaking, polishing, practising—with all the lights on the boat blazing so we could see what we were doing. In the morning, bleary-eyed, I had a shower, then plugged in my hair dryer. But, of course, there was no power. We'd used it all up keeping the lights on overnight.

So there I was, about to give a speech to 1,200 hairdressers, with no way to make my hair look good. I was ranting at my partners, "When you asked me if it was okay not to get a boat slip, you didn't tell me this might happen! And you *knew* it would!" They said, "Oh, Arlene, you're such a drama queen; just put your hair up and we'll go." I have curly hair. Really, really curly hair, and it looked ridiculous piled on my head in a poof ball, but wearing it down definitely wasn't an option. And we couldn't be late.

From the deck I could see the boardwalk, where Steve was already standing, waiting. Perfectly coiffed, of course. I asked, "How are we going to get from here to there?" In a dinghy was the answer. And my partners, God bless them, added, "Why don't you sit in the front?" I thought this was their way of apologizing, giving me the best seat. But when they turned the engine on—full throttle—I heard them snickering in the instant before the front of the dinghy lifted up, way up, and the boat shot toward the boardwalk, soaking me from head to foot. When we climbed out, Steve just looked at me, a silent head-to-toe once-over, and said, "We don't have time to fix that."

We hurried off to the hotel and I gave my presentation, very conscious of how ridiculous I looked. But I learned an important lesson that day about knowing your content. I was so glad we'd spent the night before preparing intensively, even though it resulted in a very bad hair day. We'd refined and improved our presentation, and I knew we'd truly done the best we could. Ultimately, that intensive preparation is what enabled us to persuade the hairdressers we could do something for them.

Knowing the content cold so that I could focus on responding to questions and concerns was far more important than how I looked. And if I hadn't been so familiar with the material, I might have been rattled, fatally, by the soggy lump of curls perched on top of my head.

At the end of the day, we got the contract. And, of course, something else happened at the end of the day, too: 1,199 or so hairdressers came up to me with their business cards, looked meaningfully at my hair, and said, "Honey, we can help."

RESEARCH IS A GUIDE, NOT A GOD

Crucial as preparation is to persuasion, it's simply the first step, and the only one you can accomplish on your own. Persuasion, after all, is not a solo venture but an interaction. This is why you can prepare thoroughly, cover every angle, muster an airtight argument—and yet leave the other person cold.

We've all encountered this on the receiving end of a pitch. Our kids try to persuade us to let them go to a concert, say, and they've thought through every possible objection and have a plan to cover them off. Or an interior designer unveils a detailed plan for completely redoing your living room and has priced and sourced every item, right down to the flowers in the vase. Logically, everything you're being told makes sense, and the pitcher is quite well prepared—so much so that her mind is closed to input. Sometimes pitchers have persuaded themselves there's only one perspective worth paying attention to: theirs. Whether they're unpleasantly aggressive or charmingly charismatic doesn't really matter. The issue isn't personality but inflexibility. These are the pitchers who argue with you when you ask questions and raise objections, and stubbornly insist that, with all due respect, they know their subject matter a lot better than you do.

Here's the thing: preparation isn't about setting a script in stone, but rather about suggesting a narrative arc for your pitch. You should count on the actors wanting to improvise and possibly even wanting to toss your script aside altogether. If you're too wedded to your research, you won't be able to ad lib or incorporate new input from the other side.

You want to have enough information to be able to think on your feet. But you need to have enough humility to understand that there may be quite a few things you don't even know you don't know. This is particularly important if you're trying to persuade someone to take a chance on you. Yes, you need to prove you can perform, but you also need to show you're responsive and genuinely interested in what the other party has to say.

I've had prospective clients say things like "Why should I hire you—what do you know about selling cereal? Ever sold it before?" This is not the moment to wheel out pie charts and spreadsheets displaying the exhaustive research our team has done on the cereal market. It's also not the moment to get my back up or to pretend to be an expert. It's the time to say, "No, I've never sold cereal, and I really don't know that much about cereal. I'll certainly never know as much about it as you do. But I'm interested in learning about it. And I think a new view is going to be useful to you because I don't have preconceived notions about how to sell your box of cereal. What I do know about is the marketplace and what motivates people to do things and what they look for in a company in order to build trust and loyalty." Sometimes the best way to help people get over the hurdle of your inexperience is simply to acknowledge that they know a lot more than you do about the topic. Let them be the experts because, actually, they *are.*

All the preparation in the world isn't worth much in terms of persuasion if it winds up narrowing your vision or convincing you that your expertise is unassailable. The point of preparation is not to come off as a know-it-all. The point is to give you enough confidence to open your mind and keep your mouth shut at crucial moments in the process of persuasion. Yes, shut. One of the most important steps in the process of persuasion is silencing yourself so that you can really hear the other person.

CHAPTER EIGHT

Shh!

I used to have a sign on my desk that summed up, in a single word, a little-known secret to success in business (and in life, for that matter). A lot of people coming into my office for the first time did a double take when they saw that sign, which is how I knew it was an exotic and mysterious piece of advice. Here's what it said: "Listen."

Listening is the key to understanding what other people want and need, and therefore the foundation of the process of persuasion. Sounds too simple, right? Well, though listening is something everyone can and should be able to do, many people just aren't good at it. Ever had one of those conversations where the other person talked on and on without asking a single question? Or where you had to repeat a key point—what you do for a living, say, or how many children you have—several times? Ever sat through a meeting or presentation where people doodled and checked messages until it was their turn to speak? Then you know what I mean. It's frustrating, rude even, when people don't listen. A person who doesn't appear to hear or care about anything you say isn't someone you'd choose to build a relationship with, as it would be so one-sided. And those who have the power to give you a job, or help you land a contract, or provide backing for your ideas feel the exact same way. You may be thinking, "But of course I'd listen to *them!* They're important to my future—I'd hang on every word they said."

Very frequently, however, particularly in high-stakes situations, people are so focused on their own performance that they're only half-listening. They hear the words all right, but they're not listening closely enough to process them in a way that leads to deeper understanding of the other party. Instead, they're busy self-monitoring: "What should I say next? How am I coming across? Oh no, did I actually just say that?" The only voice they're really paying close attention to is the one in their heads. If you're honest with yourself, you've probably been guilty of this yourself sometime in the last few days.

Being quiet isn't the same as listening. Even someone who's nodding enthusiastically may just be waiting his turn to speak. If your mind is actively building your own case and focusing on how to make a good impression, you can't really hear other people, much less figure out how to use the information they're giving you in order to strengthen your pitch. One of the best ways to turn off the voice in your head is simply to remind yourself that it's okay not to know everything. A pitch is not a sales spiel. It's a conversation, and the purpose is to engage and learn, not to talk and sell.

In this chapter we'll focus on the importance of turning off that interior monologue and developing better listening skills, which are absolutely vital to improving your relationships in business and every other area of life. Learning to listen is, in fact, the single most important skill you need to master in order to become more persuasive.

WHEN IN DOUBT, KEEP YOUR MOUTH SHUT

As I learned early on, even when the stakes are high, keeping your mouth closed and your mind open can be a good career move. Not long after Venture landed the account to create a co-op marketing program for hairdressers across Canada, we made a colossal error. In Quebec, based on our understanding of the English television market and a similar program we had done there, we persuaded hundreds of hair salons to sign up and pay for a television advertising plan. They committed to the program based on our promise that they would get x number of commercials for y dollars.

We proceeded triumphantly to Quebec City to ink the same deal that we had negotiated in the rest of Canada. Can you tell where this story is heading? The French television market is not the same as the English market, as better preparation would quickly have revealed. And our meeting with the major network's senior sales manager went very poorly, to put it mildly. He had no sympathy for our rookie error and told us the network would not, under any circumstances, sell us the program at the rates we had promised to the hairdressers. Then he left us in the meeting room for a moment. My partner stared bleakly out at the Quebec City skyline, then announced that if the window could open, he would jump. We were about to lose our main account as a result of not being able to deliver what had been promised and paid for. We both knew Venture couldn't survive a blow like this. Our company was dead.

It was a sickening moment, made particularly horrible because it could so easily have been averted. We just had not done our homework. I left my partner sitting there waiting to say our goodbyes and went looking for the ladies' room. It was long after hours and the station had shut down for the night. As I wandered the halls searching for a washroom, a man stopped me and asked what I was looking for.

After a short exchange, I discovered that I was speaking to the CEO of the network. So I explained why we had come to Quebec and told him that while his VP had been very kind to us, we had not been able to come to an agreement on a deal. He then invited me to stop by his office after my trip to the washroom to discuss it further.

I remember bolstering my courage as I headed into his office, which was palatial. The CEO expansively offered me a drink, and since he was drinking Scotch, I did too—I didn't really know what Scotch was all about, but I was darned if I was going to back down. The situation was completely outside my experience. I sat down, he handed me the drink, and then . . . dead silence.

I couldn't think of a thing to say or do except to approach him in the same way I'd approach any other person: with a question about his life. I asked something brilliant and insightful, like "So, how do you like running a network?" Well, he spent about an hour talking about his life and business, and I went into intense listening mode. Venture and our needs were never even mentioned. I didn't attempt to look smart, and I had no clever questions. I just listened closely and asked follow-up questions along the lines of "And how did you feel when that happened?" I was genuinely interested in his stories and his perspective, all completely foreign to me. Suddenly he stood up and said his network would make a deal with us.

When I rejoined my business partner—who'd been frantically searching for me, perhaps worried I'd located a window that opened—our career paths had changed for the better. Simply because I'd kept my mouth shut and resisted the urge to show off or beg for work.

I learned something invaluable that has served me to this day: listening and observing in an attempt to understand another person is never time wasted. Don't worry that you'll look stupid if you're not saying anything. Don't focus on what you're going to say next. Don't argue back in your head or let your mind wander. The best way to turn off the running monologue in your head so that you can really hear the other person is to tell yourself that it's okay not to know everything and not to have all the answers. Your job is to listen and really attempt to engage, so just concentrate on what is actually being said. This is your best opportunity to gain the inside intelligence that will help you be more persuasive. Simply by taking the time to put the other person first, you're creating the foundation for an emotional connection that may make someone want to do business with you.

As I've mentioned, there's a lot of research that shows that people prefer to do business with those they feel comfortable with on a personal level. Getting someone to feel at ease with you doesn't require witty repartee and dazzling verbal displays. Often it simply requires a demonstration of interest—real interest, not fake I'm-trying-to-butter-you-up interest—and a willingness to listen. Most people in the world, from toddlers to CEOs, like it when someone pays attention to them. In a one-on-one situation, many people respond warmly to someone who's asking questions and drawing them out rather than going on and on about herself.

This is particularly true if the person feels you don't have an agenda. I'm talking about trying to relate to another person and figure out what makes him tick, not trying to sell him something. I am certain that if at any point in my conversation with the network CEO I'd tried to sell myself or explain why the deal was so crucial to Venture, he would not have reversed his VP's decision. When your back's against the wall, a hard sell, particularly a desperate-sounding hard sell, is simply not persuasive. In fact, it's usually a real turnoff—analogous to an aggressive pickup line in a bar. It's always about the seller and what the seller needs, wants, and can do, rather than about the buyer's needs, desires, and perspective. Sometimes people do respond to high-pressure sales tactics, of course, but being bullied into buying a product or service usually paves the way for buyer's remorse. In the long run, no one feels good about acquiring something without being persuaded, 100 percent, of its value.

And the only way to persuade people with that level of certainty is to understand what they're all about, so you can figure out how your self-interests align and complement each other.

DON'T RUSH TO FILL AN AWKWARD SILENCE

Very often, instead of observing and listening, people talk too much, especially when they feel nervous. In audition situations, people can go into overdrive, trying so hard to impress and to show what they know that they wind up babbling. It's not persuasive, and it can be very hard to stop once you've got started.

Partly, overtalking is driven by a fear of dead air. Many people rush to fill an awkward silence, especially when they feel they have the least power in the room. A pause in the conversation is often read as a sign that the meeting is going downhill, and people respond by tap dancing furiously to try to reverse the slide. But actually, silence isn't your enemy. In fact, it can work in your favour. It can be extremely useful in terms of drawing other people out and eliciting the kind of information and reactions that will help you understand them better. If you can tolerate a lull in the conversation, very frequently the other person will step in to fill it—often by saying something he would never have volunteered otherwise. Silence has a way of making people dig deeper and reveal more.

So it's frequently a mistake to try to paper over an awkward silence with chatter. And in six specific instances, you should actively *try* to create a pause in the conversation so that you can regain control of its direction.

When it feels like a trick question
. . . .

If you're thrown by a question, don't let your nerves take over. Resist the urge to jump in with an answer. This is exactly the time to consider your response carefully. Simply say, "That's one I need to think about for a moment." Then think about it—starting with why you're being asked this particular question. What is the other person really looking for? Sometimes, people throw out an off-topic question just to see how you'll handle it—whether you'll stay calm or get flustered. The other day, for instance, in the middle of an on-air interview, a journalist suddenly asked me, "Fur or no fur?" It had absolutely nothing to do with what we'd been talking about. I paused for a moment, realized this was probably an attempt to catch me off guard, then said, "That's a very furry question."

Don't worry that taking a brief mental time out will make it seem as though you don't know how to answer the question. It's much worse to start responding with no real idea where you're headed, since you'll likely just get increasingly more rattled. Think of Sarah Palin's famous interview, the one where Katie Couric asked her which news publications she read; Palin was unable to name a single one. She rushed to answer, though she was clearly drawing a blank, rather than taking a few seconds to come up with the name of a newspaper or two. Even if she hadn't been able to remember any, she probably could've come up with something like "That's not how I get my news." Now, I'm not suggesting you're anything like Sarah Palin. You're obviously a reader! But if it feels like a trick question, pause before you answer and ask yourself, Why am I being asked this?

When someone asks a nosy question
. . . .

More than once, in the middle of a conversation, someone has suddenly asked me, "So, how much money do you have, anyway?" I've learned that when a question feels intrusive, it's a good idea to extend the pause for a few seconds before you answer. Otherwise, you may inadvertently volunteer more information than you want to, or respond emotionally rather than calmly. I count to five in my head, then say, "That's a very private question, and I'm just not comfortable answering it." If the person persists, pause again, if only to emphasize that you are taken aback, and try to force him to reflect on whether this is an appropriate topic. Then tell the truth, pleasantly but firmly: "That's the last thing I want to talk about right now. As I was saying . . ." Never feel compelled to answer an inappropriate question just because someone has asked it, whether you're in a business situation or a social setting like a cocktail party. Silence is an effective way to ensure your boundaries are respected.

When you're asked a complicated or convoluted question

Do not leap to answer a question before you fully understand what's being asked. Sometimes the question is needlessly complex because the other person is trying to sound smart. Other times, the question is convoluted because even the questioner isn't quite sure what he's asking. In either case, simply pause and say, "I'm sorry, I'm not sure exactly what you're asking. Could you please explain the question?" Getting the other person to break down the question and distill it is usually helpful to both of you and moves the conversation along. If, however, the question is still a little baffling even after it's rephrased, try to break it down into parts yourself, and answer the simplest ones first. If you're forced to think out loud, this will help you reason through the answer logically.

When you have an instinctive, negative emotional response

Sometimes at the beginning of a meeting, someone says something to me like "Wow, you're thinner than you look on TV." I used to feel offended and think, "Is that your way of saying I look fat on TV?" A few times I was so taken aback that I blurted out, "What are you saying, exactly?" I've learned to take a breath, then say something that takes the spotlight off me, acknowledges the other person's interest, and gets her talking: "I'm so glad you like the show. Are you an entrepreneur?"

If you charge in when someone makes a remark that strikes a nerve, you're likely to lead with your emotions and come off sounding brittle or hurt. So take a moment. It's possible that you've read something into the comment that wasn't there. Mentally rewind to be sure you've heard properly. If you feel under attack or that you're being put down in some way, you want to be certain you're calm when you respond. You need to collect your thoughts, so give yourself something to do—take a note, for instance, or say something that focuses outward and gets the other person talking—and wait out the pause in the conversation until either the other person volunteers more information or you're confident you can continue in a measured way.

When you're negotiating

There's a significant benefit to silence when you're negotiating, as is seen quite frequently on *Dragons' Den*. One of the dragons will make an offer, just put it out there, then go quiet. You need to let an offer sit for a minute, without explaining further and without appearing willing to move or compromise. As soon as you begin elaborating, you reveal that you're prepared to negotiate further.

You want the other person to consider what you've said and to feel that it might well be your final offer. It's not about hiding your cards but about saying, "That's my bid, and I want you to think carefully about it." The longer you remain silent, the more likely the other person is to compromise.

When you've ventured an opinion you're not sure will be embraced

After making a definitive statement of some sort, especially one that's controversial, remaining silent can confer an emotional benefit. Remember that people process information differently. Some like to sift through it very quickly; others prefer to wallow in it a bit. In either case it's a good idea to remain quiet and give the other person a chance to process whatever you just said. You don't sound anxious or overeager, and she feels she's in control because you're not pounding her with more information, telling her what to think and why. A lot of people shut down or put up walls when they feel there's too much information coming in too quickly, especially if they believe someone is trying to force a response. When you give the other person a chance to contemplate rather than pushing them forward as hard as you can, you are more likely to be persuasive.

In quite a few situations, then, particularly ones where you feel you've been put on the spot, strategic silence is often more effective than words. Frequently, too, when you're quiet, others will assume that you're being thoughtful and will be more likely to pay attention when you do speak. And, of course, when you're quiet, you create room for others to speak and to commit themselves—and a chance for yourself to listen carefully and closely, to try to figure out what's really driving the other party and what she wants.

CHECK YOUR EGO AT THE DOOR

I always know a meeting is heading south when I start feeling too eager to show what I know. If you're intent on impressing, you just can't listen closely enough. It's dangerous to go into any business situation seeking approval and applause; as soon as you're worrying about satisfying your ego, you're no longer concentrating on figuring out what the other party needs and wants. And understanding those two things is absolutely critical to being able to persuade others that the path you're advocating is the one that's right for them, too.

Your worst enemy in the process of persuasion might well be your ego. If you're concerned with proving how intelligent and accomplished you are, there's a very real risk of turning off the people you're trying to persuade. Sometimes on *Dragons' Den,* entrepreneurs wheel out fancy language rather than plain talk, flashy packaging rather than the straight goods, inflated valuations of their companies rather than sales numbers that speak for themselves. If there's too much window dressing, people start wondering why you need it and what you're trying to hide with it—even though the only thing you may be trying to disguise is a feeling of inadequacy. In any real-life situation, when the persuader seems to be overreaching and trying to sound high-flown, rather than simple and straightforward, he doesn't seem more intelligent. He just seems less genuine.

When the need for applause and acknowledgement is overwhelming, a lot of people seem to become deaf to social cues. Just think of the endless talker in your book club, the one who holds forth without noticing everyone else's eyes glazing over. Or the guy who stands up to give a toast at the party and doesn't notice that, after a few minutes, people are shifting in their seats and trying to signal that he's worn out his welcome. People like this lack the self-awareness to understand how they're coming across. They're so compelled by their desire for recognition that they don't realize how people are responding.

Again and again, I've seen good people do themselves in by insisting on their own value and trying to get others to affirm it, without seeming to notice the reaction they're getting. I think in particular of a senior executive who felt threatened when Venture was brought in to help manage a crisis that could have destroyed the organization's brand. In a private meeting, I told the executive, whose team was clearly panicked by their failed attempts at damage control, "Look, I understand you're feeling you've been pushed aside because outsiders have been hired to do what you view as your job. But if you let us help, you will weather this storm. If you try to insert yourself to claim ownership, though, it's going to be a political disaster for you because it will be interpreted as self-interest. You need to be seen as a team player who puts the company first."

This person was not untalented but insisted on getting credit and being in charge. At meetings he continued to speak up in a way I and others heard as, "I'm valuable, listen to me." Unfortunately, clamouring for respect can have the unintended consequence of persuading people you don't deserve it.

CONFIDENCE MEANS YOU DON'T HAVE TO TAP DANCE

Confidence is quiet self-belief, not a loud cry for attention. As Johnny Unitas, still considered one of the greatest NFL players of all time, defined it, "Conceit is bragging about yourself. Confidence means you believe you can get the job done." Truly confident people sit back while others tap dance. They don't need to preen and boast, or spout fancy language and complicated jargon. They're more concerned about the outcome than they are about getting credit for it. And they're better able to listen, since all their attention isn't focused on jockeying for air time.

If you don't need to fill the room with the sound of your own voice, you're free to observe the dynamics and interactions more closely. If you can stop thinking about your own need for self-gratification, it's much easier to understand what's driving other people and to figure out how to make their goals compatible with yours. At the end of the day, that's persuasion. If I understand what you want and where you're trying to go, we can probably get there together, and there's probably a way to do it that's win-win. The path to understanding is not through talking but through listening as closely and carefully as possible.

It's particularly important in a situation that's trending negative to silence the voice in your head that's screaming, "Get in there and show what you can do!" You need to keep your cool so you can really attend to the feedback you are getting instead of merely reacting to it. Even if the information isn't immediately useful, there is almost certainly something valuable you can learn—about yourself, or the other person, or the situation—that will help you next time you're in the same situation.

For instance, I was quite upset heading into the office of the Quebec network head. I thought it was very likely I'd be looking for a new job the next day, and was already mentally rifling through my list of contacts. But I knew that was the most important voice to muzzle—the one in my head that, had I listened to it, could easily have drowned out the CEO's words and wrecked my chances of learning something. I told myself I had plenty of time to panic on the plane ride home and, in the meantime, here was an unlooked-for opportunity to find out what this guy's life was like.

I recognize this may make me sound like a foolish optimist, or an optimistic fool. But just like my dad during the house fire, no matter what's going on around me, I try to view it as a learning experience and open my mind rather than shut down. If you're able to tune out the negative voice in your head telling you you've made a fatal error, or that you'd better try to save the day and show everybody how smart you are, you can remain attuned to outside feedback—and you'll almost certainly hear something that will help you in some way. You might even, as I did, get lucky and turn the situation around simply by showing that you're open to new ideas and experiences.

CHAPTER NINE

Understand

Sometimes I get the feeling that listening is a dying art. More and more, people are conducting business via email, texting, and social media—meaning that we're spending less and less time face to face, actually listening to each other. Now, I happen to love social media as a marketing tool. But while I think it's possible to promote a narrative and point of view through Twitter and Facebook, I don't think you can have a real conversation with someone via keyboard. Which is why I'm forever reminding (okay, nagging) our team to stop emailing with clients and find a way to get in front of them or talk on the phone. (Full disclosure: Perhaps the team doesn't take me entirely seriously because I'm forever emailing them.)

The trouble with email is that although it's great for communicating facts, it's not so great for communicating intentions or building an emotional connection. And remember, it's the emotional connection that's going to help you in any business endeavour involving persuasion. So unless you already have that connection, you shouldn't be trying to have a serious discussion or negotiation through email. There's just too much room for misinterpretation on both sides. We tend to read in meaning where it might not exist. A brief message can be read as dismissive and curt, when in fact maybe the sender was just swamped with work and didn't want to leave you hanging. And so on. You don't have all the additional clues to intent—facial expression, body language, tone of voice, spontaneous reactions—that people provide in face-to-face conversations.

If you're conducting your work life via email and your personal life via social media, you may forget how to listen closely to other people. This is a real problem when it comes to persuasion, where being a good listener is as important as, if not more important than, being a good talker.

Being willing to hear someone out and trying to comprehend his point of view is how you establish the foundation for trust. In today's world, where there are a million distractions and information overload is the new normal, the most valuable thing you can give to someone is your attention. Feeling that you've been heard and understood is worth so much more now because it's becoming rarer.

Really listening doesn't mean you have to provide answers and solutions. It just means you have to tune out the background noise and try to see the world through another person's eyes. Most people, even those who are standoffish at first, like the feeling that someone is listening attentively enough to pick up nuances and remember what's already been said, and will respond favourably when they see you're engaged. But you really *do* have to be engaged; it's not something you can fake (for long, anyway). Engagement is not just about eye contact and body language but about asking questions that build on what's already been said—and that show you're picking up on the subtext.

In this chapter, we'll look at why subtext is so important to persuasion and how to listen for the clues that reveal whether what's

156

driving a conversation is a desire to build a dream or a need to solve a problem. The goal is to help you listen in a different way—and to help you learn how to get others talking about the things that really matter to them, so that you can persuade them to do things your way more easily and more effectively.

IT'S A DIALOGUE, NOT A MONOLOGUE

A lot of people approach a pitch as a performance, to be followed by a Q and A session with the audience. But it's not a monologue—or shouldn't be, anyway. If you can turn a pitch into a dialogue, you greatly increase the likelihood of creating the kind of connection that will help you be more persuasive.

Your goal is to get the other person to speak first. This is not some kind of clever strategic gambit. It's just common sense. You don't want to sit and talk *at* somebody—but you can't talk *to* somebody unless you have some idea of what the other person values. So at the beginning of a pitch, I usually say something like "Since we're about to talk about something that's hugely important to you, your business, it would be great if we could hear from you first." And then I almost always ask, "What does success look like to you?" This is a tough question for many people. It forces you to step back and consider the big picture, and often people start thinking aloud as they puzzle it through. So not only is it a good conversation starter, it also gives you crucial information about what's important to the other party. And this will help you in your pitch to show how what you want dovetails with what they want.

If clients say, "No, no, we want to hear from you first," I always look for a way to connect whatever I'm saying back to them, to get input that will help me understand them. What are the hurdles to their success? What are they afraid of: competitors, internal company conflicts, falling sales? What's the thing they've accomplished that they're most proud of? What type of professional relationship are they looking for with our company? What's been successful—and less than successful—in past relationships? The more you can get them talking, the better you will understand them and the more likely you are to frame your pitch in a way that's relevant to them.

The same is true in real-life situations, too. Instead of barging ahead and outlining your grand plan for a weekend trip with friends, for instance, you'd be well advised to sound them out first, to figure out what their idea of a good time looks like (and what it costs). It's always easier to get people to open up and talk without being defensive or censoring themselves when they know you're really interested in what they have to say and aren't just waiting for your turn to deliver a monologue. And it's easier to tailor your pitch so that it dovetails with their goals if you actually know what those goals are.

There's some skill involved in keeping a conversation going, but again, it's primarily the skill of listening, very closely, so that you can ask follow-up questions that keep propelling the dialogue forward. If this isn't easy for you, if sometimes you're just not sure how to create conversational momentum or to delve beneath the surface, here's a fairly simple way to improve this skill: practise, with people you meet in everyday life. Try to listen to and draw out the person you meet at a cocktail party or when you're at the park with your kids.

As an added bonus, you might actually learn something. I subscribe to what I call the random mentor theory, which is that a mentor could be the person sitting next to you. Listen, and you will learn something—and not just about that particular person but about people in general.

THE RANDOM MENTOR THEORY

Being a good listener has a few important side benefits, not the least of which is that you will have a much more interesting life. To me, few things are more compelling than a good story, and everyone has one (though many people believe, wrongly, that theirs isn't very interesting). Often you have to coax it out of people by asking the right questions. But there's a big payoff: you find out how someone else sees the world.

Of course, understanding people is key to being able to do my job. Marketers need to know what people want, what hurts them, what brings them joy. But the knowledge—and the skill set—you can gain just from really listening to other people's stories is valuable in any line of work. And you don't need an MBA or years of training to do it. You can improve your listening skills starting right now, by practising drawing out people and absorbing what they have to say, rather than talking about yourself and broadcasting your opinions. Regardless of whether the people you're practising on are important to your career, you are developing a skill that will definitely help your career in the long run by making you a better listener and therefore a more effective persuader.

There are random mentors everywhere, ready to teach you a thing or two about persuasion—which is fundamentally all about connecting. Not long ago, I was on a plane and the young man in the seat beside mine started chatting with me. A Wharton business school grad, he'd just started working as a consultant at a prestigious firm and was engaged to marry a doctor. When I heard those three facts, I just knew I was sitting beside yet another very entitled kid who thought the world owed him success. I've hired some people like that in the past, and they've never been able to deliver. They just aren't prepared to work hard enough. But then this guy pulled out his computer and said, "I'm sorry, I really have to get some work done," and he proceeded to work like a dog the rest of the flight. As we were landing, he told me that he knew he had to pay his dues— this was boot camp, essentially—and he felt lucky to have a job at all. He'd spent a few months in Afghanistan because he wanted to understand the world a little better, and one thing he'd learned was how extremely fortunate we are to live in Canada.

He was one of my random mentors, and I think of him every time I'm in a room with someone I'm predisposed to judge. The lesson he taught me? Keep an open mind, and keep listening. You may just not really understand the other person yet.

LISTEN TO THE WORDS—AND TRY TO HEAR THE SUBTEXT, TOO

As in all relationships, in business relationships there can be two conversations going on at the same time, one spoken and one unspoken. On the surface, someone may be talking about strategy. But the subtext might be a concern about job security. Sometimes there's a significant difference between what's being said and what the person saying it is really thinking about. To pick up on the difference, you have to be listening hard, not just nodding your head and saying yes once in a while. What seem like offhand remarks are often actually indicators of subtext, but they'll fly right past unless you're really paying attention.

At the beginning of a one-on-one meeting, for instance, there's usually a pretty superficial exchange: "How are you?" "I'm okay, just tired. Never seem to get enough sleep. You?" You could respond breezily, "Oh, me too, I know what you mean" and get right down to business. Or you could pick up on it and say, "You haven't been sleeping? Is everything okay?" By pausing for an explanation, you may well find out what's been keeping that person up nights: a new baby, worry about his sick father, an old basketball injury that's flared up again. Whatever the case is, you've set the stage for an emotional connection that will help you persuade.

In the first few minutes of a meeting, there are frequently hints pointing toward these routes to connection. For example, very early in my career, before I joined Venture and was still in sales at the Calgary TV station, I walked into a meeting with the vice-president of marketing for a fairly large organization. I had no idea how to kick off. I was so green that I knew almost nothing about my business and even less about his. He was wrapping up a phone call with an insurance company, and when he hung up he apologized and explained that he'd just had a car accident. He told me a bit about the accident, how it had happened and where, but I could tell he wasn't really upset about the accident itself or the hassle with the insurance company. The way he talked about the car itself, I could tell it wasn't just a vehicle to him—it was his baby, and he couldn't stand the thought of it being damaged in any way. Underneath his professional demeanour, he was really quite upset.

I wanted to show him that I understood and could relate to how he was feeling. So I told him about my own recent car accident. My boyfriend had gone out of town for two days, kindly allowing me to drive his Porsche while he was away. This was especially generous of him, since he really loved that car. Well, I promptly backed it into a pole and wrecked the whole back panel, at which point I panicked and started phoning friends, asking where to get it fixed. Concours Auto Body, was the answer, so I drove over there. The mechanic came out, took one look at the car, and said, "Wow." I said, "Look, I know it's bad, and it's probably going to cost more than a hundred dollars to fix, but I can't worry about that now. I need you to fix it right away. My boyfriend's back tomorrow and I don't want him ever to find out about this." The mechanic just looked at me, then said, "Let me see what I can do" and went back inside the shop. After a few minutes he came back out and said, "It's going to cost $1,200, and it's going to take two weeks to get the part." I was beside myself. That was a fortune to me, and two weeks . . . ! When my boyfriend got back, I faced the music, showing him the damage and telling him I would pay for it, without ever mentioning that I'd been to Concours. He was very nice about it. A few days later he said, "I understand you got an estimate. The mechanic at Concours is a friend of mine; he just called." Apparently, the story was making the rounds, and anyone who heard it thought it was just hilarious that I figured major damage to a Porsche could be fixed in a single day for $100.

The VP I was meeting with, the car nut, laughed when he heard this, and I felt the wall come down. I knew that in his eyes I was no longer a person trying to sell him something but someone who'd understood something important about him—that he was crazy about his car. And someone who understood the sick feeling you get in your stomach when something valuable is damaged. That bond of understanding made it easy for me to connect with him, and we wound up working together until I left the station.

Now, I'm not saying it's always a good idea to wheel out a self-deprecating anecdote or in fact tell any personal story about yourself. The other person may not feel your story is at all analogous to theirs, for one thing. For another, if you go on and on, you risk looking like a narcissist. That's why it's important to gauge the reaction you're getting and be ready to course correct if it's just lukewarm.

But sometimes you have to demonstrate that you've heard the person on an emotional level before you can help him at an intellectual level. I think of business as an intellectual endeavour, but when clients also trust me emotionally, that's the brass ring.

DO THEY WANT TO BUILD A DREAM OR STOP THE PAIN?

In business, the subtext usually involves either building a dream or getting the pain to stop. Often people don't think about or articulate their desires that categorically, but if you're listening closely, it's usually apparent early on in a conversation whether you're dealing with dream building or pain stopping. If you figure out which it is, you're that much closer to figuring out where the other person is coming from—and how you can help her get where she needs to go.

Be prepared that listening for subtext is so uncommon that, occasionally, people will react as though you're a mind reader. Recently, the owner of a small but lucrative business with a very specialized market came to Venture to see if we could help him. In the course of describing his organization, he mentioned that he didn't really have colleagues he could confide in, that he felt very overworked, and just that day had been rethinking compensation because he was a little frustrated with his sales team. I said, "I'm guessing you do the majority of sales for the company." He leaned forward and asked, "How did you know?" Well, it wasn't rocket science; he'd been sending some pretty clear signals that he felt he had to build his dream all on his own and was looking for someone to help him do it. What followed was a conversation about his goals and ambitions, at the end of which he said, "You really understand me." It wasn't that hard. He'd told me everything I needed to know.

When the subtext has to do with pain people are experiencing or a vexing problem they're trying to solve, you need to be very sure you understand what's going on before trying to persuade them that you can help. Sometimes, what they're asking for and what they actually need may be quite different.

The other day, for example, an acquaintance called me for financial advice. He said, "I'm trying to build my business. It's really hard, and I'm not paying myself right now, but I feel positive because I know the wind is changing. There's some pressure on the home front but I know I can grow this business; there's a lot of work coming my way right now." And so on, for 10 more minutes about finances and structuring debt. I focused on just one thing: his throwaway line about the pressure at home. So when he finished, I said, "This has to be really hard on your marriage. You're really invigorated because you can see the opportunity, but your wife isn't living what you live. She feels terrible financial pressure because there's no money coming in, yet you're paying everyone else." He said, "That's exactly it! I don't want to put her under this kind of pressure." And then we had a whole different kind of conversation about the hardships experienced by the families of entrepreneurs, which I happen to know something about, having inflicted them on my own family. He wasn't really calling me to talk about dream building at all but about pain stopping. Because I really heard his tossed-off remark, we now have an emotional connection. He knows that I know what he's truly worried about, and that he can trust me.

Which is a golden situation in terms of persuasion. Once you figure out whether what's on the other person's agenda is pursuing a dream or stopping pain, you're better able to empathize. Being able to see what the world looks like through someone else's eyes changes the texture of the relationship.

You're also in a stronger position to persuade him of your value, as you can demonstrate real understanding. This is true, by the way, even if the other person has authority over you. People are often afraid to talk to senior executives because they're under the impression that someone so high in the food chain must be immune to emotions like fear or anger, or to chaos. But in fact, sometimes you can connect emotionally if you are able to genuinely say, "This sounds really stressful for you; is there some way I can help you through it?"

Or, if the subtext is a dream they're trying to build, "Wow, this is an incredible opportunity—what's stopping you from getting there? Can I help?"

FOCUS ON THE EMOTION DRIVING THE CONVERSATION

Venture once did a multi-stage ad campaign to try to reposition an organization in the public mind. Our client loved the first set of ads, which were high-concept and concluded with an unusual twist. Then we moved to the second round of ads, which the client approved at every stage of the game, from initial concept to scripts to the shoot. But when we proudly unveiled the first finished ad, the client didn't like it. "Where's the twist? We want that twist at the end, like last time," the executives kept saying. The Venture team understandably went on the defensive—we'd received client approval all along, we'd worked hard, there was no way every ad could have a twist, and so forth. The team took the client literally and they didn't hear the subtext, but our senior planner did, loud and clear. She said, "It sounds like you want these ads to feel unexpected, like the first set did. The twist isn't really the key issue, is it? Your concern is that if the ads don't feel fresh and unexpected, old attitudes about your organization will be reinforced." A sigh of relief on the client side—finally, someone understood! The process of persuasion had begun.

The planner was able to pick up the subtext because she didn't assume she already understood the client's perspective and she didn't react defensively to criticism. She took the time to listen, and what she heard was the anxiety fuelling the client's response to our work, which most certainly did need to be addressed.

Usually, finding the meaning behind the words requires focusing on the emotion driving the conversation. You probably already do this, unconsciously, in many relationships outside the office. You read a person's body language, tone of voice, overall demeanour. You notice if the response to a minor comment seems exaggerated, or if the person is using hot emotion words when discussing what seem on the surface to be neutral topics. You sense when you've touched a nerve. You figure out when something important isn't being said.

Parents, in particular, are genius at picking up on subtext. You just know when something's troubling your kid. Often, however, the child isn't able—or willing, particularly in the teen years—to articulate exactly what the problem is. Nevertheless, as a parent, you have the intuitive ability to get behind the words to the heart of the matter. And when you can connect the dots and figure out what's really going on, your child feels understood, which is a key part of feeling safe and secure.

In the business world, too, most people want that same feeling of safety and security, and the sense that someone is willing to take the time to understand what their work life is really like and what their business concerns and challenges are. This is true no matter how high they are in the food chain. In my experience, the more senior the executive, the higher the value placed on being understood. Bearing sole responsibility (and future blame) for decisions that change others' lives and affect a company's direction can make you feel very isolated and uncertain. Hiring, firing, arranging financing, diversifying, stripping down—these can be agonizing decisions to make and implement. It really is lonely at the top. (Having been in both spots, I know it's pretty darned lonely at the bottom, too.)

Recently, I was meeting with a CEO who was outlining an extremely stressful business crisis in a fairly dry, clinical fashion. This was clearly a stop-the-pain situation, so I said, "That sounds really difficult. I can't even imagine how you're coping day to day." The walls tumbled down. The CEO talked about the feelings of isolation and self-doubt that come with being the key decision maker in a crisis, the fear of making the wrong choice, the impact all this was having on his health. There were really two issues: the immediate danger of the crisis and the need for damage control, and the CEO's need to feel supported in developing a marketing strategy going forward. Now that I knew what was truly driving the conversation, I was in a far better position in terms of helping him. I had a better understanding of that person's challenges and perspective, and a much clearer idea of how to shape a winning pitch.

If you're able to show that you understand what a person is going through, you're in a much stronger position to persuade him that you can be part of the solution. Any business person is more likely to want to build a relationship with someone who has some understanding of the situation he's in, the problems he faces, the goals he has—and how and why he got where he is today. This is true whether the business person is a junior employee, a mid-level manager, or running a Fortune 500 company. When someone understands you, the relationship is that much more productive; you can cut to the chase with someone who's already absorbed the background and the finer points of the situation.

It may sound too simple to be true but, frequently, figuring out the subtext that will provide the key to understanding doesn't require ESP or even any special tricks. It just requires being a good listener.

GETTING THEM TALKING

If you really aren't picking up any subtext, you'll have to ask questions and probe. Gently. You don't want people to feel they've been called in to the police station for questioning. Asking from a place of understanding, where you acknowledge that you can relate to what they're feeling, is always best. This doesn't mean you have to match the other person and offer up anecdote after anecdote. Simply nodding and responding that you've been through something similar, then asking a follow-up question—"Do you know yet how you're going to handle this?"—is fine.

However, if you can't relate, there's nothing wrong with saying, "I have no sense of what that feels like; can you explain it to me?" Often what you're trying to do is get the person to finish her thought and tell you what it means to her. Think of yourself as the grade six teacher writing "Why? Please explain with more details and examples" in the margin of an essay.

I tend to ask for clarity on very simple points: "You said sales are really important, but could you clarify why they're the most important thing?" Often, driving a discussion to the basics forces people to say something or react in a way that reveals their hand. Another option is to zero in on their last point, saying, "That's really interesting. I'd like to understand that better." Don't worry about sounding like an idiot. Focus on trying to figure out how this person thinks and feels, and what they want. That's the information you'll need to be able to persuade her that you have good ideas about solutions.

When, however, my probes turn up nothing and I can't get anything out of the person other than meek sound bites, I know this isn't the kind of working relationship I want. It's much harder to engage with people who can't pinpoint what they're looking for. There's likely to be trouble down the road because either they don't have a clear idea what they want or they're simply not collaborative. I always try to keep in mind that I'm not the only person being tested in initial conversations—*I'm* also deciding whether I want this job in the first place. If someone is extremely guarded in the first meeting and you can't get her to open up or help you try to understand what she's looking for, that's a telling indication of what your interactions will look like later on. You have to ask yourself, Why is she holding her cards so close? Would I want to work with this person going forward? When there's no give and take, an emotional connection just isn't possible. Think about any friendship or positive work relationship you've ever had, and you'll see the truth of this.

EMPATHY

I'm not sure empathy can be taught. It seems more likely to me that the ability to really feel for another person is something you either have or don't have. And clearly, it exists on a spectrum. Some people are incredibly empathetic; others have empathy only for family members—if that.

What I do know for sure is that empathy is not a negative in the workplace, despite what many people believe. The conventional wisdom is that if you feel too much for others, you lack the toughness it takes to get ahead. It's just not true. In fact, if you are able to put yourself in another person's shoes, you're more likely to be able to persuade them to walk with you in the direction you want to go.

Think about it. If before every meeting you tried to imagine what it feels like to sit on the other side of the table, the meeting would probably go better. You would almost certainly be more persuasive simply because, right from the start, you'd be focused outward rather than inward. At Venture when we're pitching, for instance, we try to figure out how those on the other side of the table will feel about the meeting. Have they just sat through a few pitches and so are likely to be bored and restless? Then we'd better keep ours lively and get to the point quickly. Have we drawn an after-lunch time slot? They may be drowsy. Bringing in coffee and cookies might perk them up. Is there an elephant in the room? We'll get it on the table right away to make it less awkward for the other party and to create the possibility of a real dialogue. For instance, I knew going into one initial pitch that the president and the head of sales were at odds with each other, and also that it would be impossible for either of them to bring this up directly in front of me—so I did it for them, acknowledging that they had different agendas and needed to stop working at cross-purposes and start focusing on a shared outcome.

Taking other people's feelings into account doesn't make you less tough. In fact, it strengthens your appeal. It's just never a bad idea to consider how the world looks to the person you're trying to persuade. Usually that means you have to consider context, in the same way you would if you were trying to persuade your husband to go to the ballet rather than the hockey game—or vice versa. You'd almost certainly have better luck if you floated the idea over a nice dinner than you would if you brought up the topic in the middle of a heated argument about your in-laws. Similarly, you need to choose your moment if you're approaching your manager to ask for time off or a pay raise. Think about what that person may be going through and whether your request will feel reasonable and easily solved or like the capper to a nightmarish day.

Picking your moment means that you have to be aware of the other person's circumstances in order to know whether it's a good time or not. When my kids were young, they learned pretty quickly that it was a whole lot easier to get me to agree to something if I'd had a moment to catch my breath after work and wasn't running around the kitchen trying to get dinner on the table. If you get in the habit of listening closely and taking yourself out of the equation so that you can truly empathize with others, you'll find that good timing starts to come naturally. Empathy, in other words, will help make you more persuasive.

IT'S ALMOST YOUR TURN

You've done your homework. You've shut your mouth and really lis-tened. Now's your chance to show that you do understand the other party's perspective—which may well involve ditching your carefully prepared remarks. If you planned a spiel about strategy, say, and it turns out the client is focused on operations, you'll need to distill and reflect what you've just heard and improvise on the fly. But if you have a conceptual framework of the pitch in your head, this won't be as scary as it might sound. I know because I've had to do it myself.

CHAPTER TEN

Pitch

With any luck, the pitch you prepared hasn't been completely demolished by whatever you've learned by listening to the client and you're not going to have to come up with something entirely new on the fly. But you *are* going to have to think on your feet, since anything can happen during a pitch. Your computer, the one with the vital slide show, might crash. At a crucial moment in a one-on-one meeting, the other person might get an important call and ask you to come back some other time. During a group presentation, a colleague might make a major faux pas you can't correct in front of an audience or might forget her lines. Or the mistake might be yours. The possibilities are endless. In the early years of Venture, I'd occasionally wind up making business calls from home and, invariably, at the crucial moment, the doorbell would ring or the kids would start fighting. It's challenging to maintain a professional demeanour when teenagers are shrieking in the background, I'll tell you.

At Venture, we're pretty good at pitching, or we wouldn't have so many blue chip clients. However, we've also had some disastrous pitches, ones where you just wish you could press control-alt-delete and start over. Almost always, the issue is the unpredictability factor.

For instance, we were once invited to pitch a large U.S. retail chain. We were told the firm wanted to measure the return on its marketing efforts, which is one of our core areas of expertise, so we thought we had a real shot at this account. A small team flew down for the meeting, and when we were ushered into a VP's office to make our presentation, the mood was upbeat though a little nervous. We'd put a lot of time into our pitch and our written proposal; an account of this size and stature was huge for us. However, in our initial let's-get-to-know-each-other chat, it quickly became apparent to me that the VP we were pitching was actually interested not in marketing accountability but in something called media mix optimization, MMO for short. Well, there was absolutely nothing on MMO in our written materials. I was going to have to ad lib. Fine.

But no sooner did I start talking than the VP picked up our written proposal and began reading it. Studying it, actually. He was so intent on reading that it was a little disconcerting, but I carried on talking as he turned the pages. And then I realized, wait a sec, that isn't *our* proposal. The VP was reading another firm's proposal! After a minute or two, everyone on our team was exchanging meaningful, panicked looks; they'd also figured out that the VP was engrossed in another pitch and not paying the slightest bit of attention to ours. So one of the team members decided to try to help me out by going on at length about MMO. Just one problem: he did get the VP's attention. And it was readily apparent that my guy knew nothing at all about MMO. Still, he plowed ahead with great bravado and considerable charm. And then, the minute we left the building, he turned to the rest of us and asked, "Hey, what does MMO stand for, anyway?"

I probably don't need to tell you that we didn't win that account. (But I wouldn't have wanted it, either; I don't think I could've worked well with that particular VP.) In a pitch, sometimes the deck is stacked against you and you can't win no matter what. It's pretty likely that one of our competitors had clinched the deal before we even had a chance to open our mouths. We still laugh about that pitch today, but it's become something of a cautionary tale, too. It highlights the inherent instability of any real-time persuasion situation (and the necessity of admitting when you don't know something).

There's an extemporaneous quality to even the most carefully planned and managed pitch because it's never a monologue. It's a dialogue, but you've got only half the script—and even your half has to be tinkered with as you go. Also, the more people involved, the more improvisation there will be. Sometimes the result of all this will be synergy, and people will spark each other to greatness. Sometimes the result will just be a funny story you'll laugh about for years to come.

The moral? Anything can and will happen during a pitch, so you need to be on your toes. It helps to understand the mechanics of a pitch, which is what we'll focus on in this chapter: crafting your message, honing it, delivering it—and correcting course if you're failing to engage your audience. The unexpected will still happen, of course. But you'll have a much better idea of how to handle it.

CRAFTING YOUR MESSAGE

There are four things to keep in mind when thinking about exactly what you want to say and the words you'll use to say it. The good news: three of them can be controlled for in advance. The less good news: the very first thing you need to do requires a bit of improvisation—but if you've been listening to the other person carefully, it won't be that hard.

RECAP WHAT YOU'VE HEARD

If you've done your homework, you're less likely to be blindsided in a pitch and learn that the other person is looking for something completely different from what you assumed. And with any luck, you've been able to draw the other party out to some degree before you have to pitch. If you have, it's vital that you reflect back whatever you've just learned. Two reasons: you need to reinforce that you are a good listener, which is a persuasive quality in and of itself, and you need to check that you do in fact understand what's important to the other side. If you've got something wrong, this is when you want to find out, while there's still time to adjust and course correct.

You can't persuade someone to want to do business with you or loan you money or partner with you in any way until you persuade them that you understand what they want and need. Your aim is to weave that understanding into your pitch wherever possible and relate it directly to what you're proposing: "You talked about some of your operational challenges a moment ago, and I think our process could really help you address some of them." Don't jump to a tactical solution immediately, as you may not know the answer yet, even if you think you do. Focus instead on the process of working together to arrive at solutions.

Recapping is especially effective in everyday situations—negotiating with your child's hockey coach to change practice times, for instance, or persuading your teenager to consider a particular university—where repeating back what you've heard increases the other person's trust that you were actually listening. This makes other people far more likely to return the favour and actually listen to you, too.

So you want to illustrate that you understand and are empathetic—but you're not a parrot. While you're recapping, you can be objective and include your take on the situation. After all, one important thing you're bringing to the table is a fresh set of eyes and ears.

FOCUS ON BENEFITS TO THE OTHER PARTY, NOT FEATURES

Show that you understand what the other person wants and needs by focusing on benefits to them, rather than features of whatever you're proposing. Keep putting the other party first and viewing the proposal through their eyes. They want to know what's in it for them. Think like Nike. The company doesn't stress how breathable the shoe is or how long the insert will last—it stresses that the shoe will make you jump more like Michael Jordan. The emphasis is on the benefit, not the shoe's features.

So if it's a job interview, don't rattle off a list of everything you've ever done—talk about why and how what you've done matters to the employer. If you're pitching a widget, don't focus on all its individual components but on how it can help the person you're pitching to. If you're trying to convince your kids to stick with playing an instrument or learning a language or a course of study, don't wax poetic about the intricacies of the knowledge they'll gain or rail about all the money and time you've invested as a parent—focus on the bigger picture of how it will benefit them to keep at it.

KEEP IT SIMPLE
....

Sometimes we outsmart ourselves and overintellectualize when pitching. We come at persuasion from too high a level instead of just addressing the other person's basic need to understand what we're saying.

The other night I was reviewing a proposal with three team members before sending it out the next morning. The team had worked very hard, and the proposal sounded really smart, full of long sentences with lots of brave words. But I had no clue what it actually meant. I finally asked, "What are we trying to say, exactly?" Essentially, it turned out, we were saying that if hired, we'd help drive traffic to the client's stores. And that's the wording we went with in the end.

You can flower things up and make them sound grand, but the people you're trying to persuade don't think that way. They have different degrees of intelligence, understanding, and background knowledge, but they are all the same in one respect: they want you to demystify and simplify, so they can grasp what you're saying and weigh whether it's of benefit to them or not.

I'm not talking about dumbing things down. I'm talking about taking complex information and communicating it succinctly, in terms that people can actually understand, with no jargon or insider lingo. I remember sitting in a pitch where one of our strategists said "brand" over and over, and I could see the CEO's eyes glaze over. So I said, "You know, when I first started in marketing I had no idea what 'brand' meant. Turns out it just means your company, everything from the receptionist to the products to the core message, as seen through the eyes of others." He looked at me and said, "Oh. I always thought it meant a logo." And suddenly we could have a real conversation.

Making things sound more complicated does not make you sound more intelligent, in my opinion. After all, the smartest people in the world can make the most indecipherable topics accessible to the rest of us. Whenever I'm trying to illustrate this point, I think of the first time I met Neil Turok. Someone introduced us to each other at an event a few years ago, and we began looking for a point of commonality through small talk. He's South African, so we chatted a bit about the fact that we were both born there. I asked what brought him to Canada, and he told me he worked at the Perimeter Institute. (Actually, as I subsequently discovered, he runs it.) I had no idea what the PI was, so he explained that it's a research institute devoted to foundational issues in theoretical physics. Uh oh, I was thinking, what are theoretical physics? Neil looked equally stumped when I told him I was a marketer. We began talking about our jobs, how simple they seemed to us, and how impenetrable to outsiders.

Then a mutual friend passed by and said, "Have you asked Neil what it's like to work with Stephen Hawking?" I said, very intelligently, "What! You work with *the* Stephen Hawking?" Our friend replied, "Oh, Neil is his protege, didn't he mention that?" Well no, we had been chatting for 15 minutes by this point, and it had never come up. Neil didn't feel any need to brag. It was plenty clear that he was smart. I asked him what exactly he and Hawking talked about, and he said, "We debate the beginnings of the universe. He argues the big bang theory, I argue against it." He was able to distill his work into something I could understand, and so effectively that I felt I could ask, "How will you ever prove each other right or wrong?" A really smart person doesn't make you afraid to ask a dumb question and is able to answer it in simple terms. Neil and I have become friends, and from him I've learned about physics and also about what it feels like to do what he does. Because he's able to simplify and distill, he invites people into his very esoteric field of endeavour.

My point? If someone that brilliant can explain things simply, so can you. Speaking in plain language is a big plus when you're persuading, so keep your message simple and straightforward.

A GREAT PITCH TAKES PEOPLE ON A JOURNEY

In this world of shorthand texting and tweeting, storytelling is a dying art. But good storytelling can enhance your pitch immeasurably. The narrative you create is an invitation to others to share your view—and to connect. A great pitch invites people to go on a journey, the same one you took to come up with the ideas you're presenting. You want to take people with you, show them the process and the steps you took, how you arrived at a conclusion. If you can get them to travel down that road with you, they'll be engaged on a personal level. And they are far more likely to remember whatever you're telling them if it's presented as a continuous narrative rather than a series of bullet points.

For instance, the print production manager at Venture once came into my office very excited because he'd managed to source some paper made out of recycled dollar bills, which was perfect for one of our clients, whose business involves saving money by recycling. He told me all the steps he took to find the paper, locating the mill where it's printed, that no one else is using it—he turned the whole experience into something like a detective story, which made it totally engaging. He persuaded me to care about something I would otherwise have overlooked (and also persuaded me, by the way, that he was a dedicated employee who would go the extra mile without ever having to come out and demand recognition).

Weave your factual content into the story, of course, but there's nothing wrong with a few adjectives. People want to laugh with you—and most people are hungry for narrative. Stories present information in a lively, interesting, and memorable way, and they make sense out of disorder. Frankly, it brightens your workday to hear a good one and feel you've connected with someone.

Sometimes, it's your personal story you'll be telling in a pitch—in a job interview, say, or when asking for a raise (both are situations we'll look at in the next chapter). If so, presenting your journey rather than a laundry list of facts and accomplishments will be far more compelling. Good storytelling drives connection and makes people feel they can relate to you. Sometimes, this will require some degree of self-disclosure—why you studied archaeology but are applying for a financial services job, for instance, or that four-year gap on your resumé—which can feel uncomfortable.

But it can be extremely worthwhile, particularly in situations where you need to establish what differentiates you, or you need to make people sit up and pay attention. On *Dragons' Den,* we see hundreds of pitches in a season, so many in rapid succession that they tend to blend together. Sometimes people will say, "Remember that episode where that woman had invented such and such?" and I honestly have little memory of it.

But I can tell you, my ability to remember improves dramatically if someone has told a personal story, so long as it wasn't whiny or inappropriate, and was obviously genuine. For instance, I still remember a man who'd been a singing waiter in Italy before moving to Canada and becoming a restaurateur—and inventing an articulated snow shovel that was able to turn in any direction. He was about 80 and still shovelling his sidewalk himself. He brought a picture of himself as a young man in Italy and talked about arriving here as an immigrant. Out of countless pitches, his stands out because he told his story simply and well. More recently, there was a woman from Saskatchewan with five kids who was married to a farmer and had a photography studio on the side. I remember her because she was so hardworking and had all these other things to do, yet had found time to create a way to button socks together so the kids always had matched pairs. Her practicality and genuine manner, the way she'd tackled the challenges of starting a home-based business, stayed with me. Now, every entrepreneur has a tale about overcoming some challenge or other. Those are just table stakes, part of the job description. But the entrepreneur who's prepared to go a little deeper gets a crucial extra minute or so to try to persuade me to buy in.

Compare the appeal of this pitch—"It's a computer program to help the elderly keep track of their medications"—with this one: "I came up with this program to help older people keep track of medications because of what I saw my grandmother going through. My grandma is really the person who raised me—my mother was a single mom and she had some real struggles. Well, last year, she got ill and I could see that she was getting confused about her medications. I started to worry she'd miss doses or even overdose, but she's the kind of person who wouldn't even consider assisted living, she has too much pride. I was losing sleep worrying about her, and that's what drove me to devise this computer program, which has voice prompts, visuals, and alarms to remind her to take which pills when. It's so easy that if you can turn a computer on, you can use it. That's important with someone like my grandmother, since she's not very tech-friendly."

A well-told story makes the potential benefits of whatever you're pitching much more tangible. When you can get people drawn into the drama or jeopardy or opportunity of a situation, you're closer to persuading them. And remember, it's always okay to stumble a little and even backtrack if you have to. Authenticity is what's critical, particularly if the story you're telling is your own. Authentic doesn't mean being perfect. It just means being yourself.

That being said, be sure your story has a point and that it serves your purpose: persuasion. Long, meandering digressions just seem like oversharing, and you need to be particularly careful not to go there in everyday situations where you feel more comfortable and therefore may be more prone to divulge all. Convincing your new running group to try another route needn't involve a blow-by-blow account of your divorce from hell; a funny but mercifully brief explanation of your desire to avoid jogging past your ex's house three times a week should do the trick.

DELIVERING YOUR MESSAGE

How you deliver your message will to a large extent determine how it's received—and how you're perceived, too. But you don't need to be a mesmerizing speaker. While charisma certainly helps get people's attention, it's quite possible to be a good persuader if you're the mild-mannered type. Good delivery depends primarily on a bit of organization and remaining attuned to your audience—and ready to change tacks, if necessary.

A few words on your surroundings. If there are just a few of you in a large boardroom, don't let the table be a barrier. You can sit right beside the person you're trying to persuade, which helps make him feel you're on a par and is especially helpful at the beginning of the meeting, when you're trying to get a dialogue going. Whether the audience is large or small, when you're trying to champion your opinion, it can really help to stand up. On your feet, you have more breathing room and your voice tends to be stronger. And standing, you command attention and will feel more in control. In any persuasion situation, formal or impromptu, always maintain direct eye contact and keep your body language friendly and welcoming but not invasive or overly intimate.

USE FLATTERY SPARINGLY, IF AT ALL

When you're trying to get someone to see or do things your way, you might think it's a good idea to throw in a compliment or two

183

to smooth the path. If you really admire the person, go ahead. It's never a bad idea to show a little warmth, and a sincere compliment usually makes the other person feel good. But there's a big difference between a single, brief statement—"You've really turned this company around"—and gushing, "This is a dream come true, meeting a brilliant and innovative thinker like you." Even if that's really how you feel, it will sound over-the-top, if not insincere.

Plus, be aware that it's awkward to be on the receiving end of a stream of flattery. Sometimes when contestants on *Dragons' Den* come on set they go overboard with praise, telling us how honoured they are to meet us, what great entrepreneurs we are, and so on. It makes me uncomfortable when someone is bowing and scraping. And I always wonder why they're wasting their time buttering us up rather than just telling us about their idea. Hmmm. Maybe their idea isn't actually very good? As soon as I get on this train of thought, the contestants have a real problem: now they don't just have to persuade me to offer them a deal, they also have to reverse a negative first impression.

Often at Venture, too, job applicants lay it on a little thick, talking about how much they admire the company, what a brilliant campaign we did for *x* client, and so on. Of course, it's great to hear that people like us. But I can't hire someone who idolizes the company or me (or, more likely, is pretending to). I need to be sure that when I have a bad idea—which does, I'm afraid, happen—the people who work with me will tell me it stinks. I don't like it when I'm essentially thinking aloud—"Maybe we should consider doing *x*"—and someone acts on it as though it's an order, simply because I said it and I'm the boss. That's not loyalty. That's being scared to say no to me, which is the last thing I'm looking for in an employee.

To me, a loyal employee is someone who's always going to do what's best for our company, even if it means having to disagree with me. I want to work with people who have the strength to push back, and who have more to offer than just agreement. If you can't count on someone to tell you the truth, you don't have an employee or a business partner. You have a yes-man. The thing about yes-men is that they don't want the responsibility of partnership. And they are, in my experience, the first people to point fingers and run for the exits when something goes wrong.

This is worth bearing in mind if you're tempted, before or during a pitch, to segue into flattery. Some people, of course, lap that stuff up. But it can backfire, badly, when you're pitching people who feel secure enough that they aren't looking for sycophants.

SPEAK FROM YOUR HEART, NOT YOUR NOTES

I drive our team a little crazy because I won't let them go into pitches with a lot of notes. I think we should be able to handle an hour-long conversation without reams of spreadsheets and documents; this conveys to the client that we take their business seriously, have invested time and energy in an attempt to understand it, have internalized what we've learned, and are confident that we can handle the work.

I also don't like going in with PowerPoint presentations and endless graphics. I think they can be a crutch, and anyway, if you're fiddling with a computer and slides, you're no longer focused on the other party. When we do have to use props, we have run-throughs so the presenters won't have to look at them in the actual meeting. If you have to look at your slides, you don't know them well enough, as far as I'm concerned.

Worst of all, props get in the way of forming an emotional connection. You don't want to put anything unnecessary between you and the people you're trying to persuade. You want to encourage eye contact and create, as much as possible, a situation where you can read their body language—which is hard to do if you're hunched over a laptop.

For the same reason, I'm opposed to reading from notes: it reduces your ability to connect. I would far rather stumble over a few words but deliver them from the heart than read a perfectly crafted sentence without looking up from a piece of paper. It's pretty hard to sound genuine when you're reading stiffly. Remember, the goal is to build a relationship, and one way to get there is by speaking in an unscripted, authentic way, where you're able to focus on reactions, establish eye contact, and observe body language. It's a lot harder for people to drift off and start checking their BlackBerrys if you're looking them in the eye, speaking with a bit of passion, and sounding like a real person who sometimes muffs a word, rather than like a business robot.

This is why when I give speeches now, I almost always speak without notes—which is to say that I already know my material so well that I don't need to read my notes. Yes, I sometimes botch a line, but the quality of the connection I can establish with the audience is much richer because my focus is on them, not on some pieces of paper on the podium in front of me.

PITCH TO THE WHOLE ROOM

If there's more than one person in the room, be sure to look at and include everyone, regardless of their position. Focusing solely on the person with the most impressive title could be a major strategic error. For one thing, if only the boss likes you, you're going to have trouble even if you win. For another, you really have no idea how influential the other people are. For instance, many senior executives take their assistants' opinions very seriously. I know I do. If you ignore someone you view as "just" a secretary, you may wind up shooting yourself in the foot. In any event, chances are good that the boss will like you even more if she sees you have respect for people, not just titles. It's a sign that you're a team player who works well with others.

DON'T STEP ON YOUR OWN MESSAGE

Whatever your key point is, you want to be very sure you have enough time to say it. This is another good reason not to lead with flattery or get all flowery—if someone interrupts you or asks a question, you may never get to the point. So be sure to *spell out benefits right at the start.* These are the anchors of your argument, and you want to be sure they sink in so that even if you're thrown off course, you can steer back to them.

NOT SO FAST

While you do need to get your core message out right at the start of your pitch, you don't want to motor through your content. Anxiety can make people talk very quickly, so quickly that the audience may be lost after the first few sentences. Especially if you're well prepared and have invested a lot of time crafting your pitch, there may be some points you want to make that will strike you as so basic that you'll try to reel them off quickly. But remember that the people you're trying to persuade haven't been thinking about this topic as long as you have. They haven't been eating and breathing it, and they may not even care much about it—yet. They're not familiar with the material, and if you start rattling it off, they won't get familiar with it. They'll just feel overwhelmed.

PLAY NICELY, IT'S A TEAM SPORT

If you're not pitching solo, you've already worked out in advance who will say what. However, colleagues you've never pitched with before are wild cards. This is when you can discover that the nice guy in the next cubicle is actually a stage hog, or the woman who always seems so calm actually has paralyzing stage fright. I've learned over the years that when you're pitching as a team, smaller is better. Stacking a meeting with bodies increases the number of unpredictable variables and also can wind up diluting your message. People feel the need to justify their existence in the room by speaking up, and the end result can be confusion, not persuasion.

Even when the team is small, it's important to hammer out some rules of engagement beforehand. Most important is to establish clearly who will take the lead—and you maximize the chances of pulling off a coordinated team effort if you also clearly and explicitly establish that the lead will not get, or take, all the credit. People are less likely to feel compelled to try to elbow their way to centre stage if from the outset they know they are going to get billing no matter how many lines they have. When it's your turn to speak, be sure you use inclusive language and talk about what "we" think rather than what "I" think—unless it's necessary to take responsibility for your mistake, in which case always go with the first person singular. The goal is to persuade the other side and score a win, which sometimes means taking a hit for the team.

However, sometimes you may have to carry the meeting. Perhaps you try to pass the ball but your team doesn't catch it. Perhaps the other party is focused on a subject only you know well. Perhaps you're just talking too much. Whatever the reason, you have to acknowledge what's happening—"I apologize, I seem to be doing all the talking"— and then try to give your team some sort of role. I was recently in a

10-person meeting where a CEO brought in a team of five people, introduced them, then did all the talking himself. His team literally didn't say a word. It was extremely awkward and also distracting. Instead of paying attention to his pitch, my mind kept wandering to the same question: Why did he bother to bring anyone else along if he wasn't going to let them speak?

Alternatively, someone on your team may be carrying the meeting but floundering. Even if this is your least favourite person in the world, you must step in to help, particularly if the person is under attack: "Sorry to interrupt, but I did want to point out *x*." Or, "As my colleague mentioned before this meeting, it's very important to remember *y*." There are subtle ways to course correct that don't undermine a team member. Just don't ever leave a colleague twisting in the wind—it hurts your entire team. And ultimately, you as an individual will get more points for having someone's back. An experience I had in junior high school has always stayed with me. We were putting on a play and one actor forgot his line. Everyone on stage froze. No one prompted him, though all of us knew the line. Finally, someone in the audience coughed and I ad libbed: "Oh, listen, someone's calling us, we should all leave." And the entire cast trooped off stage! If one of us had simply whispered the line to the guy, it would have saved the entire production. Instead, we all looked like idiots.

One last thing. It should go without saying that you won't jostle for attention. But it doesn't. When people are nervous and/or anxious to establish their importance, etiquette can be the first casualty. So it's not a bad idea to say before you go into the meeting, "Let's be sure not to speak over each other. I do that sometimes, but I'm going to be really conscious not to this time." Owning the tendency is a good way to get your point across without sounding accusatory or paranoid. And then, when you're in the meeting, if someone speaks over you, let him finish. *But be sure you're heard.* You may have to insert yourself: "I do have one point I really need to make here."

It's up to you to make sure people stop and listen, and it will be your problem if you find yourself in a place of having no voice. On *Dragons' Den,* the guys sometimes talk over me; I think it's a bit of a game to them. Their voices are louder than mine, and some of them have a more aggressive verbal style than I do. But I know not to respond with irritation or frustration, which would create the impression that I feel powerless to control the situation. And I know I can't give up and just sit back. So my strategy is always the same. Stay calm, let the interrupter speak, but be certain I get my chance, too: "Wait a minute; before we go on, I have something important to say." You don't need to be loud or aggressive to be heard, but you do need to be confident that what you have to say is of value.

I do, however, have a pet peeve both about the show and the world in general. Which is that sometimes when a woman says something, it gets no response, but two minutes later when a man says the exact same thing, it's suddenly as though a choir of angels is singing. It used to bother me a lot. I'd wonder, "Did I not say it right? Was there something wrong with my wording?" And then I found out that, no, there are just people in the world who will grab on to your idea and express it. The way I look at it now is that I will still get the reward even if I don't get the credit (and that I can always improve on making sure I'm heard).

CHECK IN

You need to make sure that your pitch is actually being heard and understood, so keep checking in to see that your audience understands: "Let's just pause for a minute and look at the implication of the last point. Does everybody see why I'm saying x?" Or, "I'm not sure I'm being entirely clear. Do you follow what I'm saying?" Your tone is important; you don't want to sound condescending, just concerned that everyone is with you. Another option: "When I first tried to explain this to a colleague, he said, 'I'm not sure I get it.' So please feel free to ask questions. I know this is a lot to digest." To encourage more people to speak up, respond to questions in a welcoming way: "That's a good question" or "I'm glad you raised that." Remember, it's in everybody's interest to be sure the people you're pitching really grasp what you're saying. This is as true in everyday life as it is in business. Sometimes we think we're being perfectly clear and are unaware that other people just aren't getting it. It never hurts to check: "So if we change our club bylaws the way I'm suggesting, there might be implications in terms of our ability to attract new members. Should we go over that again?"

KEEP TAKING THE EMOTIONAL TEMPERATURE

Being able to read other people is a useful skill in virtually any situation but particularly when you are pitching, presenting, or otherwise trying to persuade others to see things your way. You need to be able to gauge their responses, so you know if you're overpowering them or mystifying them or have lost them altogether.

It's impossible to do this if you're bound and determined to stick to a script. Ever sat in a meeting while someone droned on or plowed ahead grimly, not even seeming to register the audience? You can't make emotional connections if you're not looking at people and not noticing that they've started to check their watches or have drifted off mentally. If you talk *at* people rather than *to* them—or better yet, *with* them—they aren't likely to be persuaded. They're not even likely to be engaged.

Body language speaks volumes about the level of engagement. When I'm speaking, if someone is slumped in her seat, fidgeting, not making eye contact, I can't get angry that she's not paying attention. I need to figure out how to get her engaged, fast, before I lose her altogether.

No matter how great you think your pitch is, if people are zoning out or surreptitiously texting, you need to stop and say to yourself, "This isn't working. What can I do to save it?"

COURSE CORRECT IF NECESSARY

It is possible to turn a pitch around, but you have to course correct immediately, as soon as you sense you're losing people. Chances are, you actually started losing them a few minutes ago. So don't wait, or you might not be able to get them back.

Whether the meeting is one-on-one or not, one of the most effective ways to get people re-engaged is to stop your monologue and try to create a dialogue. On more than one occasion, I've stopped mid-pitch to recap or shift gears. Sometimes it can help just to ask, "Is this making sense? Maybe we should pause for a minute so I can answer your questions." In an everyday situation, it's even easier: "I feel like I'm not being entirely clear explaining this. Am I making any sense?" Always take responsibility if people aren't following you. The truth is, it *is* your fault. You haven't kept it simple enough, or you're not telling the story very well. If you doubt this, just think about how much you learned from your favourite teacher versus the worst one you ever had—and whose responsibility you think that was.

It can also be helpful to say something like "I'm worried I'm not being clear enough. Do you mind just playing back for me what you've heard?" Getting people to play back their understanding is helpful for three reasons. First, it forces them to take an active role. Second, studies have shown that people only remember about 50 percent, at most, of what they hear (and frankly, they often hear only what they want to hear). You want to be sure your audience understands and can still remember your main points. Third, you're giving them a chance to respond to what you're proposing, which also gives you a chance to respond to their concerns.

But a light touch is important when you're pressing rewind. You don't want to come off as the stern teacher who's just decided to administer a pop quiz. Nor do you want to sound overly anxious. The goal is get the other person re-engaged without feeling he's been put on the spot, and without questioning whether he's dealing with someone who lacks confidence in her own pitch.

Another way to change gears is to recap, very briefly, your main point, then shift the focus back to the other person. If you've figured out whether he's building the dream or looking to stop the pain, you can apply that knowledge: "Earlier, you said that you want to build a Taj Mahal. I'm just wondering why?" Or, "It sounds like this company has gone through a really rough patch over the past few months. What was that like?" Asking a question is a good way to get people to recommit to the conversation.

One caveat: If you're playing to a large crowd, it's very likely that a few people will be less than enthralled. Every expert in the world will tell you not to focus on them. But I find this really difficult. I can be giving a speech to a really warm and appreciative audience, and inevitably I'll find the three who look bored out of their minds. Here's the deal I've made with myself. I'm not allowed to focus on those three because their response will throw me off, but I *can* make it my mandate to get them to pay attention—and any hint of a reaction or sign of life counts as attention. I try to view those three yawners as my challenge, but the rest of the room as my true audience. The truth is, if you've got the majority engaged, that should be enough validation that you don't start beating yourself up. Try to view the pitch as a marathon, and the three people who aren't paying attention as a blister—irritating, yes, but you have to ignore it and keep running.

A WORD ABOUT CRYING

On *Dragons' Den,* pitchers occasionally tear up or even cry. The male dragons usually have a visceral reaction. They tend to view it as a sign of weakness and say, "There's no place for tears in the boardroom, and there's no place for tears here." I view it a little differently. First off, in a boardroom, there aren't cameras. What you do and say won't be broadcast repeatedly, so that everyone from your mother to your worst enemy finds out exactly what transpired. When people cry on the show, it's not necessarily a sign of weakness. It might be a combination of nerves about the cameras, anxiety about needing money to keep their businesses afloat, and concern that everyone they know is going to see them fail. Or maybe they've allowed themselves to be vulnerable and tell us about something emotional in their lives. So if someone gets a little teary, particularly when talking about difficulties and personal challenges, I'm fine with it—so long as the person can course correct quickly. If the pitcher is in floods of tears, that's another matter. I just can't see myself partnering with somebody who melts under pressure. Weepiness persuades me to feel protective but dissuades me from wanting to invest.

In the boardroom, both men and women experience emotions in stressful situations, but they might express them differently. Men are more likely to get angry: "I told you I wanted this! Why the hell isn't it done?" Women are more likely to cry (not least because a woman who displays anger knows she may be labelled a bitch). It drives me nuts that anger is seen as a sign of strength whereas crying is seen as a sign of weakness. I think both responses are equally acceptable or unacceptable, equally strong or weak, depending on how you view the world.

Whatever your gender and whatever your emotional response, reining it in quickly is a good idea. If you get a little misty, it's not the end of the world—it may well help establish your authenticity—and making a big show of apologizing will almost certainly make matters worse. As with nerves, you now have to collect yourself and demonstrate both self-control and strength to try to get your pitch back on track. Take it from me (I've teared up more than once in business situations), it can be done. But the faster, the better.

WHILE YOU'RE WAITING FOR NEWS

In many pitch situations, you'll have to wait a while to hear whether you managed to persuade the other party. It never hurts to send a courteous thank-you note or email, but if you decide to go this route, keep it very short—your point is simply to express appreciation for getting the opportunity to pitch. If you left the pitch feeling you did pretty well but now wish you hadn't said or done one little thing, resist the urge to acknowledge it in a thank-you note. The same goes for an interview where you feel you really blew it in some way. You can't unring that bell, and ringing it again might make matters even worse. In any event, the purpose of a thank-you note is not to right wrongs or try to change someone's impression. The purpose is simply to signal that you have some manners, and to communicate gratitude that the other person made time to talk with you.

ALL THAT BEING SAID . . .
....

Persuading people who aren't sure what to do and who primarily want someone else to take a decision out of their hands is pretty easy. Persuading someone who's already determined to do something, which you believe is the wrong thing for him, is a lot more difficult. If you can get that person to see the situation in a new way and trust your vision, that's magic in business. But magic, too, is unpredictable. In the next chapter, we'll look more closely at the specifics of common pitching situations, so that you are as well armed as possible regardless of the situation. In some cases, magic is a little easier to conjure if you consider the situational variables beforehand.

CHAPTER ELEVEN

The specifics of pitching to get ahead

Even if you never have to pitch a client or get colleagues to buy into an idea, you will at some point in your work life be in a situation where you have to persuade someone. A job interview. A performance review. Asking for a raise. Asking for a chance. Asking for a second chance. The quality and delivery of your pitch is especially important in these high-stakes situations.

In this chapter, we're going to look at effective strategies and solutions you can use when your pitch has a direct bearing on your professional future. These situations feel particularly overwhelming and emotional because so much hangs in the balance. The following tips and techniques will help you to take control of situations that feel out of your control, so that you get the results you want when your goal is to get ahead at work.

PITCHING FOR A CHANCE TO PITCH

Often in life you have to lobby simply to get a chance to pitch. Maybe there are no job openings at the company you want to work for. Maybe you're looking for new clients for—or investors in—your business. Or perhaps you need to land a meeting with a senior executive at your company, someone who's so far above you in the food chain that you're not sure she knows your name or would even recognize you. Whatever the case, pitching for an opportunity to make an in-depth in-person pitch can be tough. You need to make yourself memorable—in a good way.

Trying to get an interview

Balloon-a-grams, flowers, gift baskets, camping out in our lobby, singers warbling, "Please give me a chance"—I thought I'd seen just about every trick in the book from people angling for job interviews or meetings. But recently, there was a new one. A woman turned up at our office and asked the receptionist to hand me a birthday card. I was confused. It wasn't my birthday. But then I opened the card and saw the message: "It's not your birthday, it's mine. And I'm sitting in your lobby hoping you'll see me because it's my special day." I appreciated the ingenuity of the attempt, but I didn't meet with her. And I'm pretty sure it wasn't really her birthday.

Gimmicks and big gestures just don't work with me, and I'm not sure if they work with anyone. They come off as overkill and cast doubt on your credibility—surely if you were qualified, you wouldn't need all the window dressing. It's much more persuasive and professional just to play it straight: deliver a well-crafted pitch asking for the opportunity to make an in-person pitch.

The cold call
....

"Hi, Arlene, my name is——, I've called a few times but never heard back from you. Once again, I'm an entrepreneur, I've watched Dragons' Den and done some research on your company and what you've accomplished as CEO at Venture Communications, and I hold you in high regard. I don't want to come across as a stalker, I simply wanted to get your number and give you a call to show you exactly how resourceful I am. I've had [VIP] rely on me for help, and I've dealt with [VIP]—if you want, you can call his mobile, he'll tell you what a great guy I am. Hey, if you don't toot your own horn, it won't get tooted! Listen, I don't want your money. I don't want to do a pitch. But I am starting a company with a couple of partners and just want to have a quick chit-chat with you. Maybe we could even meet some day. I hope you appreciate that when you were younger you had the same fire in your eyes as I do. I do not want anything from you, let me make that clear: I want nothing from you. I just really wanted to introduce myself. Please give me a call back this time, I'd really appreciate that. My number is——. Thanks, Arlene. Bye now."

I get messages like this one—which is a composite of several I've received recently—on my personal cell phone at least once a week, and many, many emails and letters with similar tone and content from various people who want help climbing the corporate ladder. It's really tough to make a cold call, and I'm pretty sure that people like this caller think they're demonstrating confidence and a willingness to put themselves out there. They're absolutely right. But boldness in and of itself isn't persuasive. It has to be backed by substance and a credible tone that inspires respect.

Let's look at this voicemail a little more closely, as it illustrates clearly some common pitching errors. *Hi Arlene, my name is——, I've called a few times but never heard back from you.* This opening line is a little accusatory for someone who doesn't know me and immediately puts me on the defensive, while also reminding me there was probably something about his first message that made me decide not to call back. *Once again, I'm an entrepreneur, I've watched Dragons' Den and done some research on your company and what you've accomplished as CEO at Venture Communications, and I hold you in high regard.* At this point, he needed to say what type of business he's in rather than establish that he knows who I am. I'd expect him to know if he's calling me, for goodness' sake. I think he's aiming for a respectful tone here but has veered into flattery and hasn't set himself up as someone with something of value to offer me.

I don't want to come across as a stalker. Well, okay, but . . . ! If you take nothing else away from this book, please remember that comparing yourself to a stalker or serial killer, even jokingly, is a good way to ensure you don't get a return call. *I simply wanted to get your number and give you a call to show you exactly how resourceful I am.* Digging up a CEO's personal number doesn't show that you're resourceful. It shows a lack of understanding of boundaries. And I still have no idea what this person wants.

I've had [VIP] rely on me for help, and I've dealt with [VIP]—if you want, you can call his mobile, he'll tell you what a great guy I am. A good persuader can convince me on his own and doesn't need to drop names. Besides, if these people really think he's great, they'll contact me directly to arrange an introduction. *Hey, if you don't toot your own horn, it won't get tooted!* Wait a sec. Now I'm confused. Didn't you just say the VIPs were on standby to "toot your horn"?

Listen, I don't want your money. I don't want to do a pitch. All right, then what exactly is the purpose of this call? *But I am starting a company with a couple of partners and just want to have a quick chit-chat with you.* Oh. You *do* want to pitch. So what kind of company is this, and what's in it for me? This is the heart of the matter—reciprocity, remember?—but instead of answering those fundamental questions, the caller plays it coy: *Maybe we could even meet some day.* Presumably then, all would be revealed.

I hope you appreciate that when you were younger you had the same fire in your eyes as I do. The caller is trying to persuade me by playing the similarity card, but for me, it actually serves as a reminder of my apparently advanced age and all the other ways we're different. I've never felt entitled to a callback from a CEO, not even now that I am one myself. I understand it's something I have to earn, not just expect.

I do not want anything from you, let me make that clear: I want nothing from you. But he's already mentioned a return call, a chit-chat, an in-person meeting. He wants my time, which is not nothing, and clearly also my advice, which at this point would be, "Don't make a call like this again."

This voicemail was all over the map, which immediately made me question how effective this entrepreneur would be in a sales situation. Very likely the guy just got nervous and started babbling, but the impression he left was of being unfocused and unprepared—I'm not sure even *he* knew what he really wanted from me. And I'll never find out. He may have the greatest new company in Canada, but he never told me about it or gave me a single reason to return his call. He broke the most important rules of pitching: Keep your message simple and clear, get it out early, and focus on the benefits to the other party.

Now, leaving a voicemail for a stranger is a particularly daunting way to make a pitch. You need to keep it brief; there's no time for storytelling. And there are all kinds of opportunities for things to go wrong. You launch into your message and suddenly have a coughing fit. Or your dog starts barking. Or your phone cuts off—embarrassingly enough, this happened to me twice the other day while talking to a prospective client—leaving you in a quandary. Call back and start from the beginning again? Or would that just irritate the other person? But you have no choice; you didn't get a chance to leave your phone number.

Thirty seconds into a cold call, it's quite possible to feel you've already sealed your fate. And you may well be right. Much better, in my opinion, is to send a well-crafted email or letter beforehand, so you can be sure your message is clear and controlled, and then follow up with a voicemail. Notice I used the singular: "a" voicemail. Just one. It's safe to assume, if you still don't hear anything back, that you've failed to persuade. Continuing to leave messages won't be viewed as persistent but as annoying, though you *will* make an impression—the wrong kind.

The introductory letter (or email)

Dear Arlene,

Several years ago, I started——, a business selling nut-free baked goods and snacks. My motivation was personal: my eight-year-old has a peanut allergy and had a life-threatening reaction after eating a cracker on a playdate. The parents were so apologetic, I really felt bad for them. They'd tried to do the right thing—the crackers were labelled "organic" and nuts were not listed in the ingredients, so they figured they must be safe. It just didn't occur to them that even organic crackers aren't necessarily made in nut-free facilities. And why would it? Unless your kid has an allergy, you wouldn't know how important this is.

I realized there was a real need for organic, nut-free products that taste good (I have to be honest, a lot of the stuff out there tastes like cardboard and kids just don't want to eat it). So I started my business, cooking in my own kitchen at first, and very quickly we grew, mostly through word of mouth. Today we supply birthday parties and schools all over the province, and our sales were almost $400,000 last year.

I've researched the market carefully and think there's a real business opportunity to go national. There are just no national suppliers whose products taste as good as ours. (I've sent a shipment of cookies and muffins to your office so everyone there can try them.)

Arlene, if you like our products and would be open to talking with me for 15 minutes by phone about what steps I should take next, I'd really appreciate your advice. I've noticed on *Dragons' Den* that you've backed some entrepreneurs with home-based food businesses like mine, so I know you'd have some great insights into the challenges and opportunities involved in growing my business.

In any case, thank you for taking the time to read this. I appreciate your consideration. Sincerely,———.

A letter that opens with a story is much more likely to grab me than a dry business letter packed with stilted, formal language. This one took me on a journey, with just the right amount of detail, and it wasn't overly dramatic. The message was also very clear. The writer spelled out exactly what she wanted from me—and why *me,* specifically. There was also a nod in the direction of reciprocity (baked goods are not something I'm in the habit of refusing—and sending enough for everyone in the office is a smart move, as it broadens the audience and potential support for the pitch). With a letter, too, you have much more control over your message and delivery than you do with a voicemail or a phone call, and a better chance of making yourself memorable, in a good way, to a stranger.

THE JOB INTERVIEW
....

There's so much information already out there about how to ace a job interview that I'd be reluctant to add to it except for the fact that I conduct interviews all the time so I know that quite a few people still aren't sure what to do. When you're applying for a job, the window of opportunity for persuasion is narrow, which means you have to bring your best game. But many applicants show up at our office unprepared, knowing next to nothing about our business, and seem to think that having a resumé and being willing to answer a few questions is all that's required to land a job. That just doesn't fly in the corporate world.

For a job interview, you need to go through the whole persuasion process: prepare intensively, listen quietly, try to understand the subtext, and deliver a pitch that stresses the benefits to the other party. Here are a few more pointers.

Don't ask questions that could have been answered by looking at the company's website. You're advertising that you haven't done your homework. At the very least, you should google the company and check out its website.

Do ask questions about corporate culture. "What's it like to work here? What are the values and traditions?" This is key information that will help you figure out whether the fit is right. And your questions signal a desire to fit in and contribute.

Don't slam your current or most recent employer. You risk sounding like a whiner who's not trustworthy. Even if you can't stand your job, find a few positive things to say about it—what you've learned, how it's helped you grow.

Do tell the truth if you were fired from your last job. The correct wording: "I was fired." Be as straightforward as possible when explaining why you lost your job, what you did right and wrong, and what you learned from the experience.

Don't rely on flattery. It makes it seem as though that's all you have to offer.

Do try to get the interviewer to talk about her dreams and aspirations. "What do you like about working here? What kind of people would you like to have working here?" Any questions that create a real dialogue promote an emotional connection and also elicit information you can weave into your pitch.

Don't blame other people for the state of your career. You will come across as a person who doesn't take responsibility for your own life. In interviews I often ask whether someone is lucky or unlucky. If the answer is "I'm unlucky because all these bad things happened to me," I know the person doesn't hold himself accountable, so I won't be able to, either.

Do be prepared to give a detailed answer to the question, Why do you want to work here? Something vague like "It's a great company" just isn't sufficient.

Don't say, "I want to work here so I can position myself to move to x company." Why would someone sign on to train you and invest in you if you're already planning your exit?

Do stress the benefits to the company if you're hired, rather than the features of your resume. Employers want you to show them the forest, not the trees. At Venture, we interview many recent graduates who don't have any marketing-related work experience. Some try to compensate by focusing on the strength of their academic credentials: "I have a BA from McGill University, and a 4.0 GPA." Which is great, of course, but we need to understand what you learned that might help us—and quickly, because there are 30 other qualified applicants for this job.

Here's the kind of pitch that gets our attention: "In my final year at McGill, I participated in an interesting research study on creative collaboration in ad agencies, and I think what I learned from that study could help you here. Let me tell you a little bit about it and how the findings are relevant to your company." We've hired graduates with degrees in English, commerce, philosophy, science—fields with no connection at all to what they actually wound up doing for us. But they persuaded us that what they learned at university would give them a fresh perspective on our business and add a layer of complexity and uniqueness to the company. Benefits, not features.

Let your personality shine through

People tend to get hung up on trying to say the right things in a job interview rather than trying to make an emotional connection. This is one reason the conversation so often is stilted and the situation feels so uncomfortable.

It's been drilled into us that we need to be very disciplined and linear, but what's more useful for an employer to know is how you think. And what's more useful for an interviewer to hear is your singular voice. Dutifully parroting phrases from the website—"You say you want x, and I am x"—won't make you stand out. Letting your personality shine through will.

The most engaging interviews I've ever had are the ones where the applicants have demonstrated passion and authenticity. I remember a young man coming in to see me who said, "I have no experience." But he had tons of energy. He was like a puppy dog, jumping at my heels. Then he said, "Listen, I have to tell you about this idea I have for a commercial." I can still remember it today. He said, "There's a ship, think about the *Titanic,* going through the water. It's foggy, the captain's at the deck trying to navigate, the foghorn's sounding, there's a huge iceberg ahead. And then suddenly the captain pulls out some Windex, sprays it on the window and can see—so the *Titanic* is saved! What do you think?" I looked at him and said, "Tell me how *you* think, what you see when you have ideas—words or pictures?" He said, "I see pictures; I can see the story in my mind." This was a decade ago, maybe more. So I said, "Okay, I'm going to hire you as a receptionist." I didn't have any other jobs available, but I knew I wanted someone with that kind of creativity and energy at Venture. He did very well here and is now the creative director at MuchMusic.

Actually, some of the best hires I've ever made have been people who couldn't be shoehorned neatly into a position—sometimes I didn't even have jobs for them yet—but who nevertheless persuaded me they would bring something valuable to the company. They all shared a sense of self-assuredness in the way they presented themselves. When I hear passion and personality shining through because someone is really able to convey what drives and motivates him and how he views success, I'm highly engaged. And if he can link all that back to my organization, even better. Then we're able to have an actual conversation rather than a job interview.

You may have more to offer than you think

Many people have more marketable skills than they realize. Running a household, organizing your finances, juggling school and work, volunteering—think about all the managerial and time-management skills you learn from life experiences and how they could be of use in a workplace. Personally, I know that no business school can teach you how to prioritize, delegate, motivate, and defuse high-conflict situations as effectively as motherhood can.

It's very persuasive when people are able to frame skills learned in one area as assets in another. It shows that they're self-aware and are thinking about reciprocity and what you need, not just what they want, right from the start. For example, one young woman with a degree in sociology who was working as a receptionist recently sent us a really effective cover letter. It wasn't "I have terrific clerical skills and a university education." The thrust of the letter was that both her academic background and current job had taught her a lot about how to read people and communicate effectively—skills that are critical in marketing. Instead of apologizing for working as a receptionist when she was qualified to do more, she persuaded us that her work experience would be a plus to us if we hired her to work on marketing campaigns.

Frankly, her willingness to work as a receptionist despite her qualifications also impressed me; it's a good indication that she's a hard worker who doesn't view any job as beneath her (and yes, she got the job). I'm willing to answer phones or photocopy documents or do whatever I have to to make our company a success, so I'm looking for people with a similar world view.

If someone's only a 4 out of 10 on a skill set but a 9 on common sense and good judgment, I'll hire her. I can teach someone a skill—but I can't teach common sense and good judgment. I know because I've tried. Either you have them or you don't. And an initial encounter, whether it happens via a voicemail or a cover letter or an in-person meeting, is an opportunity to demonstrate that you do. It takes good judgment to figure out what the other party wants and needs, and it's just common sense to stress how you fit the bill.

MOVING UP THE LADDER

Landing the job is only the beginning, of course. Very likely, at some point in your career, you will have to pitch for a raise or a promotion. Some people feel they shouldn't have to do this, that good work should automatically be noticed and rewarded. In an ideal world, it would be. But in a lot of workplaces, if you wait for someone else to recognize and escalate you, you'll be waiting a very long time. Ensuring you get what you believe you deserve will require you to pitch.

Asking for a raise—what not to say

Most people dread asking for a raise. So much so that some never do because it just feels too pushy. They sit back hoping for better compensation and may take it personally if it never arrives.

Sometimes, though, the reason is simply that the boss is preoccupied and doesn't see the disconnect between the quality of your work and the size of your paycheque. I'm sorry to say I've been guilty of this myself. I've commended people for doing outstanding work but have failed to reward them with a raise. I don't do it on purpose. I'm just distracted by some other business challenge and don't make the connection.

Unfortunately, I don't think I'm unusual in this regard. Because your boss is in a position of power, you may think she's in control, but chances are good she's spinning, too, and you're not her number one priority. If your good work isn't being noticed, it may not be purposeful. It may be the same as when your husband doesn't notice your new haircut—the boss is oblivious, not purposely trying to hurt you.

At least once in your working life, then, you'll probably find yourself in the situation of trying to persuade someone to give you a raise. But many people feel so nervous—or, alternately, so resentful that they even have to ask—that they forget all about the concept of reciprocity when they're pitching. They may feel they've already given the boss plenty and don't have to prove how the company has benefited from their presence.

I've been pitched for raises many times, so let me start by telling you what doesn't work: coming at it with a chip on your shoulder and an aggressive attitude; approaching the situation apologetically, as though you really have no right; or barging into your boss's office rather than scheduling time beforehand. There are some commonly used arguments, too, that are less than persuasive.

I need a raise because my rent went up/my daughter is going to private school/I'm buying a house. I'm interested in my employees' lives and I want to know—and help, if I can—when they are suffering in some way. But wishing you had more cash to bankroll your lifestyle doesn't qualify as suffering. This isn't my problem (and frankly, it's not very persuasive in any business setting to point out that you have trouble managing your finances). Always make sure that what you're trying to get others to do is lined up with their interests.

If you don't give me a raise, I'm going to quit. I always say the same thing: "Goodbye." Ultimatums and threats really do not work. They breach any emotional connection that might exist.

I have another job offer but haven't accepted yet. I'm torn. I have a standard answer for this line of reasoning, too: "You should take the offer." Just one exception to my rule: if someone has been head-hunted and is being considered for a very different role from the one he currently holds in my company, I'd take the time to find out more and to see whether a similar role might be possible with us. But if someone went out on my time and actively sought and interviewed for another job, the truth is, he's already gone. He's no longer committed to my company. It's been a very long time since I've matched an offer, and I wouldn't do it today because it just doesn't work. I don't think you can recover people who've gone so far as to send out resumés and interview with other companies. You just can't count on their loyalty anymore. My feeling is this: if you're unhappy or unsatisfied, come to me first. Let's talk before you start filling in job applications.

I've looked at the market, and the job I'm doing is worth x dollars. Three issues here. First, I may not be able to pay what you think the market is offering for your skill set, and second, your opinion of your job performance may be quite different from mine. Third, when you're thinking about compensation, you have to consider the whole package—benefits, salary, working environment. It's possible that you could be paid more elsewhere but would hate working there.

Asking for a raise—what you could say

Here's a good, though not perfect, approach: "I think I've really contributed greatly to the company this year and would like to talk about a raise." Of course, you need to have substantive proof of your contribution, by which I mean concrete examples. Remember to stress benefits rather than features (more on this in Chapter 10), or you'll get bogged down in details. Since you'll likely only have a few minutes to make your case, you want to be sure that the boss sees the big picture.

Here's an even more persuasive approach: introduce the concept of reciprocity and future benefits. The reality is that you've already been paid for what you did last year. It will take you further to point to what you're planning to deliver this year. Give some examples of how you've already proved your value, then outline what *more* you can offer. In other words, explicitly point out what's in it for the company if you're given more money.

But sometimes the company simply can't afford to pay you more. In which case, if you want to continue working there, it's fair to say, "I know times are tough, but would you consider giving me extra time off in lieu of a raise?" You may have to be a little creative to come up with something that works for both parties.

One final note on this topic. Remember that if you haven't had a performance review in a while, it may not be an indication that your manager doesn't value you. It's more likely that he's dealing with the fire on his desk and simply isn't thinking about how long you've been waiting. In which case, here's a line of persuasion that's worked on me: "I've done a self-assessment, highlighting what I think I've accomplished in the past year and where I think I could grow. I'll leave it with you but would love to get in your calendar at some point for 15 minutes to get your input."

SEEKING A PROMOTION

The best way to persuade a manager that you deserve to be elevated is to punch above your weight in whatever job you're in now. If you're not only doing your work well but actually passionate about a job you know you're better than—well, that's your best possible pitch right there.

A few years ago at Venture, we had a receptionist who was super organized, upbeat, and helpful, both noticeably bright and personable. Exactly the person you want at the front desk, in other words. But after a few months, our creative director came to me and said, "I'd like to try her out as an apprentice in our department." She had no formal experience in our industry, but her raw talent was recognized because she was willing to give 150 percent to a job she acted like she owned. Her attitude wasn't "I'm stuck in reception; this is a temporary thing." Quite the opposite. It was because she did her job so well that it became clear she deserved an opportunity somewhere else. She's still with us, by the way—as an awesome copywriter.

People who demonstrate passion for their work, coupled with a willingness to learn, get considered for other roles. The best way to get a promotion is to be highly competent at your current job while also demonstrating that you're a learner who's seeking knowledge outside your area of expertise. That's what will make you attractive to an employer—much more attractive than if you announce that you've been clocking in for a year now and therefore deserve a bigger title.

To get unstuck, you need to be willing to take risks

With any luck at all, you're in a workplace where merit is recognized and rewarded. But perhaps you aren't. Perhaps you're doing an outstanding job, and maybe everyone around you even recognizes that you're striving for excellence, but still . . . you're stuck. Getting yourself unstuck may require a gutsy move. The truth is, if you've made yourself invaluable in a support role, but you want more, it may not happen unless you're willing to take a risk.

One option is to go to your boss and start by acknowledging her contribution to your success to date—not to flatter her but to remind her that she's invested in and will get credit for your future success:

"You've been a good mentor and given me a lot of opportunities. One thing you've taught me is the importance of continuing to challenge myself." You want your manager to feel she's playing an active role in keeping you in the organization, only in a different capacity: "I love working here because I've learned how to do *x* and I really enjoying doing *y*, but I feel I need new challenges and think I'd be doing myself a disservice if I didn't actively pursue them." Remember, if your boss really likes you and doesn't want to lose you, she'll do whatever she must to keep you. You don't need to deliver an ultimatum—as I explained earlier, these usually backfire anyway—but you could say, "Over the next six months I want to be trying to transition to a new role, and if I'm not, I'll have to start thinking about moving on." That's not a threat, but you are putting the manager on notice that you're intent on getting out of your rut.

I understand this is a scary proposition. But many people are capable of so much more than they're currently doing. The issue is being afraid to dream big. They don't feel they deserve anything better than what they have now. And this is where self-persuasion comes in—and can be a negative force or, depending on how you channel it, an exceptionally positive one.

We're told that to have a meaningful career where you feel you have some control over your destiny, you have to have had a special and privileged start. Many people are convinced that success is connected to your genes, or growing up with a silver spoon in your mouth, or having a diploma from the best institution, or knowing the right people, or having a powerful mentor—and that these things are for a special few, not for the rest of us. This is one myth I really hope my own story has persuaded you is untrue. Yes, you need to have some core competencies and an appetite for hard work and for learning, but the main qualities you need are tenacity, perseverance, and faith in yourself. It's that complex and that simple.

So how do you get noticed? In business, you have to believe that if you work hard, conduct yourself ethically, are supportive of and help create a positive corporate culture (we'll talk about how to do this in Chapter 13), you will be rewarded. So if you feel disgruntled because you're not being elevated yet others are, you need to take a good hard look at yourself to see why a leader isn't bringing you along. Sometimes it's because it's the wrong leader. But in a large organization, there are enough levels of leadership that, if you're doing excellent work, you should get noticed. So just maybe the problem is you. Maybe you've failed to persuade the powers that be to pay attention. And if that's the case, you need to understand why so that you can learn from your mistakes.

That's what we'll focus on in Part V.

PART FIVE

YOU WIN SOME,
YOU LOSE SOME

The pitch is over, and you know how it was received and whether you were persuasive or not. So it's time to move on, right?

Not just yet. There's still one more crucial step, and that is taking stock of what went right, what went wrong, and what you could do differently next time. Becoming more persuasive is an ongoing project where you're always learning and can always improve. In the following chapters we'll look at ways to reframe losses and wins, so that you learn from both. You'll develop not only more self-awareness but also more self-confidence—both of which will help you next time.

CHAPTER TWELVE

The trouble with losing

Sometimes I've walked out of a pitch with a sick feeling in my stomach, knowing we don't have a prayer. Other times I've left on a real high, certain we're going to land the account. In the first case, I don't think I've ever been wrong. In the second, I definitely have been—we've failed to win some accounts where I thought we'd knocked it out of the ballpark. Either way, losing doesn't feel good, though it's hardest to accept when you've mentally placed yourself in the winner's circle. Then you can torture yourself, wondering, "Why? The meeting went so well. What went wrong?" It's especially difficult to answer this question when actually, upon review, you can't imagine things going any better than they did. You're pretty sure you did everything right.

And maybe you did. But even when things go perfectly, you can't always manage to persuade other people to give you what you want. They may have been looking for someone older and more experienced. Or someone younger and cheaper. Perhaps your presentation really was very good but another candidate's was even better. Or maybe the other candidate had an inside edge: he went to college with the interviewer—or had a picture of the CEO in a compromising position. Chances are, you'll never know for sure why you didn't win.

In my experience, the feedback or explanation you receive won't be very helpful. At Venture, we've heard it all: "Your agency is too big." "Your agency is too small." "Your approach is a little too edgy for us." "We're looking for something a little edgier." And so on. Generally, the explanation you're given isn't the real reason. It's a little like dating. No one ever says, "Look, I don't want to see you again, so I took the time to jot down a detailed and brutally honest list of everything I dislike about you. Consider it my parting gift." What people say when they're just not interested is "It's not you. It's me." Or some other nonsensical platitude that doesn't leave you feeling enlightened and doesn't give you the information you need to avoid making the same mistakes again. Instead, you're left still puzzling over what, exactly, went wrong.

As with dating, when you fail to land the job or the account or the promotion, or fail to get others to buy into your idea or support your proposal, the real issue may well be a lack of chemistry. The fit just wasn't right. Think about it. Just about anything else can be fixed, at least in my line of work. They didn't have confidence in the account manager? No problem, we'll get another one. Didn't like the creative work? Fine, we'll fix it. Didn't like the price? Let's talk. The one thing that probably can't be fixed is a failure to connect.

Chemistry, that sense of an emotional connection or the possibility of one, is so important when you're pitching. Many times, selecting a winner from the shortlist will come down to a single question: Who would I rather work with more? If they didn't choose you . . . well, that's life, and beating yourself up over it won't help.

In this chapter we'll look at the consequences of failing to persuade. How you respond to the experience will determine whether it's destructive or constructive—yes, constructive. If you're able to deconstruct your pitch, identify your mistakes, and frame an appropriate response, losing can be one of the best growth opportunities you will ever have.

BE A GRACIOUS LOSER, EVEN IF IT WASN'T A FAIR FIGHT

I'll never forget the time Venture won a new account and we were summoned by the client to meet with the previous marketer at a restaurant. He'd been working with the client for about 10 years, and the client's idea was that he could bring us up to speed on their business. A friendly meeting over lunch, it was thought, would ease the transition.

Well, the marketer who'd lost the account didn't share this vision. He showed up at the restaurant late, dropped an open banker's box on the table and pushed it towards us. It was practically empty—it held only a few videos and a very thin file of notes. "That's everything I've got," he announced ungraciously, then left. It was horribly awkward, not to mention unprofessional. After a decade of working for a client, you generally need a team of people and a bunch of wheelbarrows to transfer your files. While I could empathize with his disappointment about losing the business— been there, done that—he still had an obligation to the client who'd been paying him for so many years. And he owed me a little professional courtesy, too.

The marketer's lack of graciousness ensured that he'd never work for that client again and that he couldn't use them as a reference— which, if you lose graciously, is still a possibility in many cases. It also ensured that he and I would never work together.

And that's my point. You never do know what might happen in the future, which is one reason it's a bad idea to burn bridges when you lose. In the future you may well encounter the person who handed you your walking papers in another context. Or maybe there will be a turnover in management and you'll have another shot at joining the same company—so long as someone there doesn't remember you as being a sore loser. Or perhaps someone at the company will go out on her own and start a new business, one you'd be perfect for. You remain a contender for future work if you're able to leave the ring with the same dignity and poise you'd show if you won.

Last impressions are almost as important as first impressions. Remember, you are playing a long game, and the real thing that's at stake is not a particular job or piece of work but your reputation. Your reputation is your strongest currency in business.

Depending on the situation, you might consider sending a brief note to the person who didn't give you the job or the account. The message should be along the lines of "Thank you for your time; I appreciate your interest in me. I wish you and your company continued success and hope our paths cross again in the future." Losing graciously while reaffirming that you still have an interest in the organization shows class, confidence, and integrity.

PERFORM AN AUTOPSY

All of which is not to say that a failed pitch is a festive occasion and you should be dancing in the streets. My point is simply that responding with defensive anger or self-flagellation won't help you improve next time. And all it will do this time is prolong the pain of the loss. When you fail to persuade, the most productive response is a post-mortem. Analyze your mistakes so you can learn from them. Give yourself a day or so to cool down and get over the disappointment, then really try to be objective about your pitch.

Maybe, in fact, there *was* a problem on your end. If there was any-one else in on the pitch or presentation, get together to deconstruct what happened. Instead of complaining about the horrible injustice of it all, try to analyze your performance objectively to help figure out why you lost. If you pitched solo, you should do the same. Instead of stew-ing, revisit the process of persuasion as clinically as possible to see if it broke down somewhere, and how. Did you prepare adequately? Were you really listening, or were you overtalking? Could your message have been sharper and simpler? What about your delivery?

Be honest with yourself about what you could do better next time, then figure out how to improve. Every mistake should be viewed as an opportunity for future growth. For instance, if you think the issue was nervous babbling, start practising listening more closely—not just at work but everywhere else too, as explained in Chapter 9. Consciously focus on keeping your mouth shut and hearing what other people are saying each and every time you have a conversation, whether it's in the boardroom or at the supermarket checkout. It's amazing how quickly you can train yourself to be a better listener.

If, in retrospect, you decide the problem was that you stepped on your own message, try redoing the pitch (in front of a mirror, if necessary). Walk through it again to figure out how you could have done it better. Don't endlessly rehash the conversation with your boss or your child's teacher or the hotel manager who refused to give you your money back; there's no point in getting upset all over again because things didn't go your way. Focus instead on what you could do differently next time, and on whether you were attending closely enough to the subtext of the interaction.

Remember, self-awareness is the goal here. The more mindful you are of your weaknesses, the more likely it is that you'll be able to overcome them or compensate for them in the future. Just think about what you'd say to a child who didn't make the team: "Don't take it personally. Practise so you get better, and maybe you'll make it next time." It's good advice.

DON'T PERSONALIZE FAILURE (EVEN WHEN IT'S PERSONAL)

Because an emotional connection is so important to persuasion, there's no getting around the fact that sometimes when you lose, the problem wasn't external and there weren't errors in execution. To put it bluntly, the problem was you. The decision maker wanted to work with someone else more than she wanted to work with you. There might be something about you that's viewed by 99 percent of people as a positive but, for some reason, rubbed her the wrong way. The only thing you can control is your response. Don't take it to heart.

Um, you're thinking, how could I *not* take it personally? Because it was, in fact, a rejection of me and my personality. You're right. But if you were authentic and honest and did nothing wrong, and still someone didn't warm to you—well, thank God you didn't get the job/the account/the opportunity. It's not enjoyable or comfortable to work with people who don't particularly like you or who aren't on the same wavelength. When the emotional connection is non-existent or negative, it's not going to be a highly productive, energizing partnership. It's very difficult to do your best work with someone who really doesn't enjoy being in the same room as you.

This is something I know first-hand. Over the years I've learned there are some clients who just don't want to work with me. They don't like my style, my personality, my solutions; but fortunately, they do like Venture. So I've removed myself from their accounts. Which isn't to say that it feels good to be disliked. It doesn't. But the fact of the matter is that not everybody gets along, not everybody can be friends, not everybody likes each other's styles. Sure, you want to try as hard as you can to make an emotional connection, but there's no point turning yourself inside out trying to win unanimous approval. If you did, you'd no longer be authentic. You'd be a chameleon, focused on pleasing at any cost.

A thick skin is essential to a happy life—and the more success you have, the more you will need one. You can't imagine how many letters and emails I get from *Dragons' Den* fans, critiquing everything from my hairstyle to my intelligence to my facial expressions. While it's a lot more enjoyable to read love notes than hate mail, I can honestly tell you that these kinds of criticisms bounce right off me. My sense of self-worth doesn't come from strangers' approval, though of course it makes me feel good when I do get it.

All that being said, if you're getting consistent negative feedback about your performance at work, it's time to consider whether there's some merit to it. If the same complaints keep surfacing from different sources—"too passive," for instance, or "not a team player"—it's a good indication that you need to look at what you're putting out there. Part of self-awareness, after all, is knowing how you're viewed and why— and ensuring that others' perceptions align with your own understanding of your personal brand. If, for example, people don't like working with you but you are getting ahead anyway, is that how you want to be viewed? For some people, the answer is yes. In which case, terrific. But if the answer is no, and there's a big difference between how you see yourself and how others see you, it's a sign that you need to re-evaluate your personal brand, as the essence you *think* you're putting out there is clearly not what others are perceiving. And the same goes for everyday life. If you find you're not getting the kinds of social reactions you're hoping for—people duck your calls, friends don't exactly jump at your invitations—maybe it's time to re-examine your personal brand.

REFRAMING HOW YOU THINK ABOUT LOSING

You have to believe what you're doing is valuable and worthwhile, even if others don't think so. Your sense of purpose and self-worth is your best armour against the pain of rejection. Frankly, if rejection is going to throw you off course, you probably don't belong in the business world, and you're going to have a tough time in the rest of life, too. There are few guarantees in business, but one is this: You will miss out on a job or a promotion or a new client at some point in your career. It happens to everyone, even the most charismatic and charming and talented people in the world.

Rejection isn't fatal, professionally. But your reaction to it could be. We all know people mired in bitterness over career failures who never recover and can't move on. Equally trapped are the people who became so frightened by one misstep early on that they resolve never to make another, and let one good opportunity after another slide by. Sometimes, a rejection opens the floodgates for old insecurities to come rushing back. You might start questioning whether you're good enough or smart enough to succeed. If so, you need to rethink your version of success.

In business—or any other field, pretty much—your version of success has to be generous enough to let you weather rejection without feeling like a reject. I define success qualitatively rather than quantitatively; the money I make is just a by-product, not the end goal. For me, success is not just about making deals and growing our company. It's primarily about doing interesting work as well as I can and having a full life with as many new experiences as possible (and new experiences bring new risks of failure). Consequently, I don't have the same drive to win at all costs that some of the real superstars in business have, and sometimes I will be passed over as a result. But that's okay. I can deal with rejection because it's actually woven right into my idea of success. And my knowledge of the business world.

MAKING MISTAKES IS MORE HONOURABLE THAN ATTEMPTING NOTHING DIFFICULT

We teach kids that mistakes are learning opportunities, yet many adults conduct their work lives as though making a mistake could be a potentially career-ending blow. The truth is, mistakes are an inevitable part of the equation of achievement. To make a mistake, you must have taken a risk of some sort. And a willingness to take risks is honourable and courageous (so long as they're not stupid ones, like driving too fast or turning up drunk for a meeting).

In fact, as my dad taught me growing up, a life spent making mistakes is more honourable than a life spent attempting nothing difficult. If you try to avoid all situations where you might make a mistake, you run the greatest risk of all: winding up with a dull life and a lot of regrets—not to mention a shortage of anecdotes about your setbacks. When I sat down to write this book, I realized that most of my favourite Venture stories revolve around our mistakes, which still make me laugh. And, occasionally, cringe.

In the early days, most of my missteps involved being penny wise and pound foolish. Any entrepreneur who's not well funded knows the kind of mistakes I'm talking about, the ones where you scrimp on the wrong things and wind up causing trouble for yourself. When Venture was in its infancy, my four partners and I worked for two years without really taking salaries and relied on lines of credit, their personal savings (I didn't have any), and credit cards to bootstrap the growth of the business. To paint you a picture of how little capital we had, in the early years, we rented space in a building on a month-by-month basis. It was month to month, as the building was scheduled for demolition. The elevator didn't work and we were on the sixth floor of this mostly empty structure, which was made of wood. This is a key point for the story, trust me.

One of our clients, a restaurant chain, had asked us to develop coupon books, which the printer then sent to our offices for storage until the distribution date. It was the first major printing job we had undertaken and we did not appreciate the volume of books we'd created. When a semi backed up to the building with a few tons of coupon books on board, we had to come up with a plan for storage. Fast. So I had the bright idea that we could use the floor below us to store the books. It was empty, who would care? We unloaded the books ourselves—they took up the majority of the space on the fifth floor—and congratulated ourselves on saving a bit of cash on storage.

Several days later, a knock on our door. It was a guy from the legal firm on the fourth floor. He was wondering if our ceiling was starting to cave in the way his was, and whether we should call the landlord to investigate. Of course, we said no and told him not to worry, it was probably nothing, then proceeded to rush down to the fifth floor and move all the books out. Because the floor was so precarious, we had to crawl over to the boxes commando-style. There were four or five of us creeping the way you'd move to rescue someone who's fallen through thin ice, dragging the boxes out.

Some mistakes make great stories years later. Others never seem funny. But persuading yourself that it's all right to make them, that in fact mistakes are necessary for growth both in business and in life, is a crucial step in persuading yourself that it's all right to try new things and to take risks. To move forward, you have to make mistakes.

HOW YOU THINK ABOUT YOUR
MISTAKES INFLUENCES FUTURE PERFORMANCE

A couple of years ago I read an article in the paper about kids and motivation. It quoted an expert who thinks it's a bad idea to praise kids for being smart. Apparently, it can backfire, so that kids become afraid to make mistakes. That made a lot of sense to me because of my own experience in school. Being told I was smart made me really scared to fail, and I just stopped trying.

So I went online and found some of the studies mentioned in the article, which provide compelling evidence that how you think about mistakes plays an important role in whether you succeed or not. Carol Dweck, a psychologist at Stanford University, has spent more than 30 years researching how our beliefs shape our perception of events. She found that a "fixed mindset"—believing that talent and intelligence are genetic and can't be changed—makes you more likely to fear failure and less likely to take on challenges. But a "growth mindset"—believing that intelligence can be transformed through effort—makes people much more inclined to try their hand at tough tasks and to view mistakes as learning experiences.

Here's why your mindset matters: *it actually influences how well you perform.* People with a growth mindset, who think it's okay to make mistakes once in a while, tend to outperform those with a fixed mindset. The reason is not that they're more talented but that they view mistakes as learning opportunities rather than failures and are more inclined to keep at something until they succeed.

In other words, the story you tell yourself about your mistakes really matters. If you tell yourself you can't change the hand life dealt you, you tend to see one failure as the final verdict on your ability: "Clearly, I'm just not good at sales; that's why I didn't make my numbers. I'll throw in the towel now before I make an even bigger fool of myself." If, however, you believe in your potential for transformation, you're more likely to try again, since you view failure in constructive terms: "Hey, what can I learn from this? How can I improve?"

You may be wondering how knowing any of this helps you if you already have a fixed mindset. Doesn't that mean you're already sunk? No. You can change your mindset. I know because I did it. There's also scientific proof. As one of Dweck's experiments demonstrates clearly, a mindset can be established or altered in a very short period. She gave fifth graders a set of puzzles to solve; when they received their scores, regardless of how well they actually did, the first group of kids was praised for being smart, and the second group was praised for having tried hard. Next, she gave them a choice of taking an easy or hard test. Two-thirds of the kids who'd been praised for intelligence opted for the easy test—they didn't want to lose the "smart" label, while 90 percent of those praised for effort opted for the tough test, apparently wanting to hang on to their reputation for trying hard.

Then Dweck administered a test so tough that none of the kids could pass it. The ones who'd initially been praised as smart were more likely to give up and decide that, actually, they weren't smart at all. But the children who'd been praised for effort stuck with the test longer and didn't lose confidence in themselves. Finally, she gave both groups of kids a test that was identical in difficulty to the first one they'd taken. The results were dramatic. The scores of the kids who'd initially been praised for intelligence declined 20 percent, while the results of the kids praised for trying hard increased by 30 percent.

This study and many others paint a clear picture. If you view setbacks as learning opportunities instead of failures, you will actually perform better long term. So how you frame your narrative around mistakes matters.

YOU'RE IN GOOD COMPANY: HIGH ACHIEVERS ARE MISTAKE MAKERS

Virtually all great scientists and inventors view mistakes as necessary steps in the process of creation. Consider Thomas Edison's perspective on his unsuccessful attempts to invent the light bulb: "I didn't fail one thousand times. The light bulb was an invention with one thousand steps."

Something I find helpful to bear in mind when I mess up is that even the most extraordinarily accomplished people have experienced failure, sometimes over and over, before achieving anything of note. Henry Ford had a few companies that were history before the Ford Motor Company made history. His take? "Failure provides the opportunity to begin again, more intelligently." Walt Disney's first cartoon production company went bankrupt. (And, by the way, if it weren't for his wife's brilliant suggestion, Mickey Mouse would have been known as Mortimer Mouse.) As a 22-year-old, Oprah Winfrey was fired from her job as a reporter by a producer who deemed her "unfit for TV." In her words, "I only got the opportunity to co-host a talk show because I had failed at news."

Mistakes, failure, adversity—they're all wonderful teachers, so long as you focus on the lessons to be learned rather than the disappointment to be experienced. And setbacks can intensify the hunger and the stamina required to achieve, as well as helping to temper brashness and erase arrogance. This is why some business leaders look for employees whose resumés include a flop. Sir Richard Branson, for example, has managers within the Virgin organization who might have been overlooked by other companies because of failures earlier in their careers. At Virgin, errors on the job are valued as long as you learn from them.

The proven ability to come back from a mistake is something I also look for when hiring. When I'm interviewing to fill a position,

233

I'm always more interested in how people have handled trouble, and what they learned from the experience, than in where they went to school. Managers who can acknowledge their mistakes and recover from them are exactly the kind of people you want to partner with because they won't fall apart when things don't go according to plan (which is something else you can count on in business).

IF YOU CAN'T ACCEPT THAT YOU'VE MADE A MISTAKE, YOU MAY MAKE AN EVEN BIGGER ONE

Very few people score a home run—or even manage to avoid striking out—their first time at bat. My first entrepreneurial venture, the gift basket company I started with my sister-in-law, could not be characterized as a win. We also with great enthusiasm invested in a company that printed names on ribbons, so we could customize the ribbons that decorated our baskets. Let's just say it wasn't my smartest investment.

But I sure learned something about getting a company off the ground. I learned that you can put all the passion in the world into what seems, sitting at your kitchen table, like a surefire moneymaker, and it still may go nowhere if the market is simply too small or it's impossible to make a profit. Or maybe it's simply a bad idea. I also learned that, at a certain point, you have to accept the market's verdict and pull the plug, regardless of how much money and energy you've invested and regardless of your belief that the project should have worked.

Sometimes, though, people just can't let go of that belief. And you do hear really inspiring stories about people who lived in their cars and stubbornly held on to their dreams and wound up achieving them. You also hear stories about ideas and products that were rejected over and over—the Harry Potter books, for instance, and the earliest Apple computers—but went on to huge commercial success. But that's not how the story ends for most entrepreneurs who can't pull the plug on a failed venture. Much more frequently, they wind up broke. There's a fine line between holding on to your dream and losing touch with reality.

To me, this is the most heartbreaking aspect of *Dragons' Den.* Again and again, entrepreneurs tell us that after failing to get traction in the marketplace, they decided the solution was to sink yet more money into their kitchen gadget or board game or whatever. It's not uncommon for pitchers to have invested their entire life savings into something that we, and viewers at home, can tell instantly is a dud. Often there's simply no market for these items, but the hopeful entrepreneurs just couldn't believe or accept that they'd made a mistake. Instead of putting the idea on the back burner or trying to launch it again at another time, they continued pouring in time and effort. Perhaps they didn't have enough faith in themselves to believe they'd ever have another idea.

THERE WILL BE OTHER OPPORTUNITIES

People who are able to admit they've made a mistake, then cut bait and move on, usually *do* come up with other ideas. And according to a study conducted by a group of economists at Harvard University, serial entrepreneurs are more likely to succeed than first-timers. Clearly, they learned something useful from their failed ventures, something that helped them the next time out. And there's more. Failed serial entrepreneurs are even more likely than successful serial entrepreneurs to get funding from the same venture capital firm that financed their first venture. The first project might have bombed, but they did learn how to persuade backers to stick with them. In business, that's what we call a success.

After a failed pitch, don't persuade yourself that you just blew your last chance in life. The reality is, there's opportunity everywhere. Along with problems, there's potential on every path. So you will almost certainly get another chance to succeed. That's why you need to pick yourself up, figure out why and how you missed the mark, and strive to improve. Dwelling on disappointment and failure won't help you win next time.

BITTERNESS IS NOT AN OPTION

There's a quote by the mathematician Blaise Pascal that I love: "Bitterness is like drinking poison and waiting for the other person to die." Even when you haven't just lost but have actually been denied something you've earned, there is absolutely no point in continuing to feel angry or resentful about the injustice. The best course of action is simply to take the lesson, incorporate it into your approach going forward, and move on.

For instance, the same company that ordered all those coupon books when Venture was just starting out couldn't pay the printer's bill. Nothing we said or did could persuade them, and taking them to court would have cost more than we could've won. So Venture wound up paying every penny of the bill, which as I recall was in the neighbourhood of $80,000—a fortune for a struggling new company. We had to pay it off in instalments. But stiffing the printer wasn't something we even contemplated. We all understood that business is a long-term game and that making a subcontractor eat the loss would come back to haunt us.

We gave ourselves a day or two to feel really pissed off, then we dusted ourselves off and hit the streets looking for new clients. And we took the lesson from our mistake: Be careful who you trust. The truth is, we'd ignored some troubling signs about that particular client—lateness with payments, for instance—and they'd convinced us we had nothing to worry about. We wanted the business so much that we convinced ourselves none of that mattered and so ignored our gut instincts.

The sad fact is that in business, as in life, you will run into unreliable people. Some will persuade you with promises—"I'll pay you back at the end of the month"—they have no intention of keeping. Others will be gifted liars expert at figuring out how to push other people's buttons. This is why you have to listen very intently when someone is telling you what you want to hear, and remember to pay close attention to your instinctive reactions, as discussed in Chapter 1. They're usually an excellent guide to helping you figure out whether someone might have less-than-honourable intentions.

Allowing yourself to sink into bitterness, whether it's about a mistake or a loss or an injustice, will not help you succeed next time. It will only sour you and make it more difficult for others to feel they can—or want to—connect with you.

FOCUS ON LESSONS LEARNED

As I've said, you won't always be able to persuade others, not even if you follow every single piece of advice I've given you. The unpredictability of the dynamic and the infinite variables in play when you're dealing with other human beings make it impossible to create a formula that delivers guaranteed results.

But you do have a framework now for thinking about persuasion, and for thinking about mistakes. They don't kill you. If you respond to them properly, they can help you develop so that you do better next time. And if you keep losses and mistakes in perspective and view them as learning experiences rather than irreparably damaging events, there will be a next time, I promise.

CHAPTER THIRTEEN

The trouble with winning

You got the job, or the raise, or the promotion, or the new client, or the capital infusion for your struggling company, or whatever it is you were trying to persuade someone to give you. Congratulations! Celebrate your success and enjoy the moment. But just for a moment.

When you win, you should go through the same post-mortem process you do when you lose. What went well? How did you manage to hit the right notes? And what went wrong? What could you do even better? Here's a bracing thought: maybe you were just the best of a bunch of pretty weak contenders. You'll want to be stronger than that next time, when the field of candidates may also be a lot stronger. So analyze your pitch just as you would if you lost. Sometimes analyzing a winning pitch can be even more useful. When your confidence hasn't taken a hit, you might see your performance more clearly and own up to missteps more readily because you know they didn't have negative consequences. And chances are, you'll figure out something not just about yourself but about the person you persuaded. In retrospect, you might realize something that winds up being useful going forward; maybe you'll remember a throwaway remark you didn't pay much attention to at the time, or perhaps you'll recognize a conversational theme that didn't strike you at first. If it was a group effort, you may find others came away with a different take or noticed different things than you did. It's worth taking the time to review what happened, not as an exercise in self-congratulation but as a learning opportunity.

Now that you've won, you need knowledge about the other party more than ever. Because here comes the hard part: you have to deliver. As everyone finds out sooner or later, persuasion *does* come with a cost. Accountability. Once you've convinced people to give you what you want, you'd better be sure you deliver. Sometimes it's easy. You can manage the bigger job or the new project with no problem. Making operational changes turns out to be even simpler than you imagined. Reaching a new sales target is well within your ability. But sometimes what you promised to do is exponentially more difficult than you imagined it would be. (And if so, you'll want to think about changing the way you prepare for and research your next pitch.) Which is why you need to be selective in terms of how you go about influencing people to do things. Chances are good that you'll have only one opportunity to ask someone else to join you on a particular path, so you'd better be really sure you can—and want to—deliver.

Below, we'll look at some of the typical challenges that accompany delivery: dealing with criticism, difficult people, office politics. Viewing these challenges through the lens of persuasion, and approaching them using the process you've just learned, can help you overcome them rather than being overwhelmed by them.

DELIVERY IS A FUNDAMENTAL OBLIGATION

Principled persuasion always implies an obligation to other people, particularly when it involves convincing them to give you a chance or do you a favour. It's a little like politics: if you talk people into voting for you but don't do what you said you would, they won't be voting for you again.

For instance, very soon after I became CEO of Venture, when we were still quite a small firm, I heard through the grapevine that other agencies were pitching the Alberta milk producers. We'd never handled an account of that size, but I called the milk producers' VP of marketing and asked if we could pitch. She said, "I'm sorry, but we've already determined the list of firms we'd like to have compete." Then she added, "Besides, I've never even heard of Venture. Why aren't you even listed in the Yellow Pages?" This was 15 years ago, when a Yellow Pages listing was as important as a website now. But the importance of a listing in the Yellow Pages had honestly never occurred to me, as I admitted to her. Then I said, "I just need to ask you one thing. What have you got to lose by including us on the list at this point? I know it's a couple of hours of your time, but if you'll just give us this chance, I promise we'll make it worth your while. You have my word that we will not waste your time. And maybe we have a better approach than the other firms on the list."

I think she could hear the conviction in my voice. I truly believed that bigger firms didn't have some kind of magical ability we lacked, and I'd persuaded myself we could compete at their level. But getting the chance meant (very politely) not taking no for an answer.

You really have to be listening closely to figure out the difference between an absolute no and a no that means maybe. Don't push if someone has said, "Absolutely not." But if the person has indicated uncertainty or is willing to engage in a discussion about her reasoning (as the marketing VP did when she mentioned that we didn't have a Yellow Pages listing), that can be permission to push. There are no hard and fast rules here, because much depends on the subtext, the person's tone, and the overall tenor of the conversation. But so long as you're polite rather than aggressive and obnoxious, it may be worth a try, particularly if there's a big upside. The bottom line is that tenacity and persistence are part of the equation of success. I've met a lot of talented people who've never quite managed to translate their talent into business success, and very often the explanation is simply that when they reached a hurdle, they sat down instead of trying to jump over it. Their perspective is, it's impossible, why try? My perspective is, it's improbable, but why not at least try?

Apparently the milk board VP had the same world view. She thought about it, then called me back and said, "Okay, I'm persuaded. If there's any chance of finding a better solution for the milk producers by expanding the search, then it's my obligation to do that. I'm going to let you pitch." Having convinced her to step outside the box, I felt a huge sense of responsibility to put together a terrific pitch, to show her she hadn't made a mistake. We were nervous, but I'd promised. And when you've promised, and someone has taken a chance on you, you have an obligation to go to the ends of the earth, if necessary, to deliver. So I hired Terry Belleville, an award-winning creative director, to help ensure that the calibre of our pitch would match the work I knew we could deliver. And we worked round the clock, literally, to come up with a great presentation.

I'll never forget standing at the front of that hotel room in Edmonton, facing a U-shaped table with about 15 major dairy farmers plus milk board staff. We'd drawn a bad time slot—right after lunch, when everyone was a little drowsy—so we'd brought chocolates and cookies, hoping the sugar would wake them up. I was as nervous as I've ever been in my life, but Terry and I just pitched from our hearts, and we knew we'd come up with the best possible concept we could. I also knew I had nothing to lose and everything to prove—particularly to the VP I'd persuaded, who was there in the room, watching. I wanted to win the business, of course, but an equally important motivator was my feeling that I owed her. I didn't want to let her down.

That's the thing about persuasion. When someone puts enough trust in you to give you the go-ahead, they've given you the keys to their kingdom, and you have a responsibility to try your hardest to deliver. If you blow it, you have to go down knowing—and showing—that you gave it your all. We won the dairy farmers' business, coming out of nowhere, and worked with them for eight years. Of course, persuasion was just the first step. After that, it was all about producing the results we'd promised. Which is why, when you set out to persuade someone of something, the true measure of success isn't winning. It's whether you won and could actually deliver.

RESPONDING TO CRITICISM

In business there's no such thing as smooth sailing. There are always going to be disagreements and bumpy patches, just as there are in any relationship. And as with your personal life, how you navigate through the tough times will either deepen your connection or fracture it.

As you begin following through and trying to deliver, whether that involves increasing profitability or meeting a sales target or showing that you can perform in a new role, you'll almost certainly find yourself in even more situations where you'll need to be persuasive. Now, however, you won't be pitching to win new work. You'll be responding to criticism and trying to persuade people they were right to be persuaded by you in the first place.

View criticism as a challenge to do better
....

Almost inevitably, there will come a moment when you are told that some aspect of your performance or delivery could stand improvement. Sometimes the criticism is unfounded. But sometimes it's absolutely fair, once you look at the situation through the other person's eyes. In any event, all post-pitch criticism deserves serious consideration, as it may provide the key to delivering on what you promised.

Venture works with one large organization that issues an annual report card, rating its contractors and consultants on a variety of measures, and one year we got a really lousy grade. The remarks on the report card verged on scathing, and the team immediately became defensive—the client was difficult, the deadlines were impossible, and so on. I had a different reaction. My first response was "They're really unhappy, how did I miss this?" My second response was disappointment in myself and the team. We are in a customer-centred industry and job one is to keep our clients happy. Blaming the client is always my very last response.

So I told the team that we could condemn the client and lose their business, or we could weigh their comments and try to think about the relationship from their perspective. The truth is, it's very difficult to give honest criticism. It's really hard to be the critic, which is something to bear in mind when you feel under attack: this isn't a happy moment for the person who's criticizing you, either. This is a tough situation for both parties, and that's something you share. When someone feels compelled to take on the unpleasant task of being brutally honest, you need to at least consider that there may be some validity to what he's saying.

We all stared at the report card for another minute, then a senior planner said quietly, "I think it's much more fair than we want to believe." That broke the ice. The tone in the room shifted rapidly to one of constructive self-criticism. It could easily have continued as a bitch session, with everyone concluding that the relationship was impossibly broken and there was no way to fix it. But instead, the team came up with a plan to turn things around based on the client's input, to fix the specific problems that had been noted, and to get as much information as we could about what else we could do to improve.

It worked. We kept the client, and the next report card was outstanding.

Criticism can be an opening to dialogue

In everyday life, many people shut down or lash back reflexively when they're being criticized. The response is instinctive, and connected, I believe, to an unwillingness or inability to listen when you feel you're under attack. But this is one circumstance where it's particularly important to listen closely, as these types of conversations almost invariably have a rich subtext that can help you understand the other person better—even if, in the end, you decide his criticism is unfounded. Remaining calm, closing your mouth, listening carefully, reining in your ego, recapping—all the tools of principled persuasion can be used to your advantage in situations where you're being criticized, and they will get you closer to a resolution, faster, than just about anything else you could do.

As in life, so in business. If a client tells me, "I hate the ad campaign you came up with," I can view this as an attack or as an invitation to debate and defend the merits of the campaign. Or I can view it as an invitation to a dialogue that is going to help me better understand the client's needs—and help the client better understand the path I think is right for both of us. So I always choose the latter route.

245

Criticism is often a signpost that someone's off track, and it might well be me.

That's why my first response is never to treat it as an assault of some sort, even if the wording is harsh, but as the beginning of a discussion that could wind up being really helpful. At worst, it's a learning opportunity. The most important task is to get as much information as possible before you react or respond. If the criticism is broad and sweeping, you want to get the other person to elaborate and provide as many details as possible: "I'm sorry you're unhappy. I want to figure out what went wrong, and fix it. Can you tell me specifically what you dislike about the campaign?"

It can be really difficult if you feel you've been ambushed, but keep your tone calm and your body language relaxed. No crossed arms, no raised voice. This is all part of business, and everyone's been through it—including the person who's delivering the criticism.

In fact, this is another persuasion situation. Now you are pitching for a chance to make things right. So you need to go through the process again. First, shut up—muzzle the voice in your head that's angry or afraid or indignant. Then *listen*. While the other person is talking, don't formulate your rebuttal or muster your arguments. Try to hear what he's saying as well as what he's not saying, the subtext. Probe for more information if you don't feel you understand why the other person is dissatisfied. In this situation, it's particularly important not to rush to fill an uncomfortable silence. Remember, your silence helps draw the other person out, and you need to find out as much as you can about what's driving the complaint before you open your mouth to respond.

And when you do respond, remember that you're in persuasion mode. Start by recapping: "I understand you're not happy with the work. What I'm hearing you say is that you think it's too drastic a repositioning of your brand." Your message is simple: "Obviously, we want to make you happy." Try to take the other person back through the journey that brought you to this point: "Can we take a few minutes to go back over the process so we can figure out together where it broke down? One of the key findings in our research was x, and then focus groups confirmed y. In our meetings with your team, we reviewed all of this and decided z."

It's important to remind people of the journey for several reasons. First, you can't count on them remembering every step. Chances are they haven't been living and breathing it the way you have. Second, it will help you dissect the criticism, understand it better, and convey your understanding to the other party. Third, you're reinforcing that this has been a shared process—one that may have broken down, yes, but one that you didn't initiate solo, and one that earlier they agreed to and are therefore invested in.

If there's some obstacle to delivery or some external explanation for your performance to date, now is the time to mention it: "I understand that you think my report was not fully informed, but here's some information I can share with you about the data. Are you open to hearing why section two was framed this way?"

Timing is important. You need to be sure the other person has had the opportunity to have his say, and that you've had the chance to show that you heard clearly and understood, before responding. You also want to try to weave your understanding of the criticism into your response. It's important to avoid blaming language—and to be concise: "As you mentioned, there's been some disagreement about how we should roll out the ads, regardless of their content. So we should talk about some of the challenges we've been facing in terms of getting buy-in from your marketing team. It would be really helpful to get your input."

Finally, emphasize your accountability. You don't have to be servile. Just keep it simple: "I'm going to figure out how to fix this in order to deliver what I promised. I am going to make this right. Thank you for taking the time to review it with me."

When responding to criticism, focus on benefits, not features

Sometimes you know the criticism is justified. When you think about it, you have to admit that you really *have* been late to work pretty much every day. You just didn't think it was a big deal. Or you really did do a slapdash job on that last report. You just thought it was so minor that it didn't really count.

When you find yourself in the position of having to acknowledge that, upon reflection, you can see your critic's point, view your apology as a form of persuasion. You're pitching for a second chance. Start by silencing the voice in your head that's already apologizing and really listen to the criticism so you can recap it. Then, your message is simple: "I'm sorry, I really didn't understand how important this is to you, but I do now. And I'm going to show you I can improve. I'm going to fix this problem—here's how." Or, if you don't know how yet, say so: "I acknowledge that this is a real issue, and I'm going to figure out how to solve it by the end of the day. I'll check back in with you so you know exactly what I'm going to do."

The fewer excuses offered, the better. What your critic wants to hear about are the benefits to her: your apology and your solution, essentially. The features—your explanation for your missteps—are irrelevant. If you can apologize and propose a solution, then deliver on it, that says a lot about you as an employee or vendor. Demonstrating that you can take direction and change your behaviour accordingly might actually wind up improving your working relationship with your boss or your client.

Own your mistakes
....

One of the most important tests of character at work and in life is how you conduct yourself when you know you've made a mistake but no one else has found out yet. If there's ever a time to speak up and be honest, this is it. I can't think of a scenario where it wouldn't be best to be the first to acknowledge your error. If you wait until it's discovered, you run the risk of looking like you don't recognize or accept that you did anything wrong, or like you've been trying to conceal it.

As an employer, I respect the person who comes to me and says, "I'm sorry, I messed up. Here's exactly what I did, and here's how I'm going to fix it." You need to acknowledge your issue, persuade me that you have it under control, and assure me it won't happen again. That takes guts, and I award points to the person who can do it, so long as she also has a solution and follows through on it. It says volumes about a person's integrity as well as her ability to deal with challenges and solve problems.

I need to be clear that being honest about having made a mistake doesn't mean providing a blow-by-blow analysis of *why* you made it. The why is much less important than how you're going to fix it, and long-winded explanations tend to come off as attempts to shift blame and avoid taking responsibility. Details about your personal life are particularly problematic. There's little anyone else can do about your personal problem, for one thing, and for another, you run the risk of sounding like you're bidding for sympathy, not apologizing and troubleshooting. If you need time off to deal with a particularly stressful situation at home, simply say so, with a brief explanation. Anything more is too much information. Most persuasive to me is something along the lines of "I let my personal life get in the way of my performance, but my reasons don't really matter.

What matters is that I didn't do what I was supposed to. I want to fix it, regain your trust in me, and let you know that I'm aware this is not my shining moment." As a boss, it's pretty hard to find fault with that.

There's no such thing as an employee who makes no mistakes. So the best employee is the one who makes the occasional mistake, promptly owns it, and corrects it.

Of course, I make mistakes too, plenty of them, and one thing I've learned is that small mistakes in business can turn into really big problems if you don't immediately acknowledge and try to repair them. In my experience, it's rarely a major faux pas that costs you an account. It's the little things. There's a tendency on the client's part to interpret small errors as indicative of a larger problem in the relationship, which is why you have to move quickly to address them rather than take the attitude that the other party is just nitpicking and in the end will see the big picture.

Recently, a client who has been clear that she's very happy with Venture's work told me how unhappy she was that we'd assigned a new person to help out on her account without consulting her first. She was still dealing with the same main contact, mind you, and the new person was performing well in an auxiliary role, which is why to us it didn't seem like a big deal. But she was absolutely right, we should at least have communicated with her beforehand and explained our rationale. When I apologized, she said, "I appreciate that you're admitting you made a mistake; let's carry on."

The lesson: Everything can be going very well, but one little error can become like a rapidly spreading cancer that threatens the entire partnership. What seem to you to be a few minor, unrelated mistakes can come to seem, in someone else's mind, like related events that speak to the quality of the relationship.

GROUP DYNAMICS

Rarely, even if you're self-employed, will you find yourself delivering on a pitch in complete isolation. Almost always you're going to have to report to and/or work with others in some capacity, so delivery will require dealing with other people, some of whom may not be people you'd choose to partner with if you had any say in the matter.

I remember sitting in meetings early in my career, nodding and trying to be agreeable while thinking, "I can't work with this person." And then having to work with that person. The reality is that, just as not everyone will like you, you're not going to like every person you work with. Some you won't even be able to stand. But you'll still have to find a way to work with them. Even trickier, you may well find yourself having to persuade them that the two of you can work effectively together. This is when being a good listener will be vital, and when, more generally, the process of principled persuasion can help see you through.

When others view you as a threat

Sometimes when Venture is hired by a company, it's clear from the outset that some people on the inside find our presence threatening. Usually the issue is that they want to protect their turf and are worried that we're going to take over their jobs and start ordering them around. Occasionally, they feel the presence of outsiders is humiliating, equivalent to a company-wide announcement that they can't do their jobs properly. The key to success in this situation is to figure out other people's agendas, what they're looking to achieve, and what they want, and then take their objections off the table as quickly as you can. The end goal is to persuade them to work with you so that you can deliver.

For instance, we were once brought into a small company that prided itself on making everyone who worked there feel like part of the family. The in-house marketing team, however, made us feel that we were unwanted relatives. In our very first meeting, then, their agenda seemed obvious: they were determined to prove to the CEO that they didn't need a marketing firm. So our job was to persuade them we had no interest in taking over. My message was simple: "We're going to give you everything you need to be stars in this company, so that a year from now, we won't be here. You won't need us anymore."

When there's an elephant in the room, it's always better to try to put it on the table and deal with it in a straightforward manner. It may take some courage, but it's far less stressful than trying to muddle through in a poisonous atmosphere, pretending there's nothing wrong. In a situation where people feel fearful, you can diffuse hostility rapidly simply by addressing their fears directly—then persuading them to focus on the benefits they will get as a result of working with you. Again, the process starts with listening. Put your own opinion aside and try to find out what they're feeling and truly understand where they're coming from. Really try to understand how the situation looks from their perspective. When you do this, it's easier to figure out how to respond.

In my experience, one of the best ways to deal with naysayers is to give them credit for success whenever possible, while still being honest. This is challenging, as focusing on a fearful or negative person is a mistake, in the same way that focusing on the three people who aren't paying attention to your speech is a mistake, because it might throw you off course. But if the naysayer is a key stakeholder who has the leader's ear, it's crucial to develop a relationship and persuade him that your presence is going to help him in some way. One good way to start is by giving him credit, as publicly as you can.

I know, I know. It sticks in my craw too sometimes, to be generous toward someone who's treated you with suspicion and distrust. But ask yourself, Do I need all the credit? Or can I share it with someone else who frankly does deserve credit, in order to accomplish my ultimate goal, which is delivery? You can count on one thing: the person you give credit to is not stupid. He'll know you made him look good. And trust me, this will make him want to keep you around more, not less, and your working relationship will almost certainly improve. You may never be friends, but you *can* create a more productive modus vivendi.

When you're delivering, but no one seems to notice

In every office I've ever set foot in, there's someone who's viewed by co-workers as a climber who hasn't paid her dues. Sometimes the person is actually managing pretty well in her role and is trusted by management. Nevertheless, there's a consensus that more deserving colleagues have been bypassed, and that the person's promotion was unfair.

This may well be true. But let's consider how it probably happened and what you can learn from it, which will help you more than feeling resentful ever could. In my experience, the person who's viewed as a climber tends to be someone who knows how to manage up. She makes a point of alerting her manager to any good thing she does and, yes, sometimes implies that she played a larger role in achieving a positive outcome than she actually did. Well, her boss is busy, tired, and likely doesn't know the facts (people always think the boss is far more aware of everything than he really is). He's dealing with the fire on his desk, and in walks the climber—having paved the path for a while by pointing out her triumphs and all the challenges she faces—to ask for a promotion. Sometimes this request is accompanied by a threat, explicit or implicit, that if she doesn't get one, she will, regretfully, have to leave the company (as I mentioned, this doesn't work with me, but I know it does with some managers). If she hasn't been trouble to her boss, and if her boss is unaware of her colleagues' feelings, the attitude is generally, "I need to make this problem go away and get back to the fire on my desk." This is, in a nutshell, how some people, including some undeserving ones, get ahead. They build their own portfolios, rather than helping to build an organization, and they do not sit back and wait to get noticed.

Here's the bad news: the climber is actually a good persuader who's better at pitching to higher-ups than her peers are. The good news is that if she's completely undeserving, she'll be caught eventually—but it's easy to hide in a big company, so it may take a while.

Instead of waiting for vindication, why not try to move forward yourself? You can start by learning from the climber's pitching techniques. There's no reason you can't employ them ethically, to ensure that the powers that be know about your accomplishments, too. Instead of sitting back modestly and hoping someone will notice when you pull off a success, view it as a persuasion opportunity. You could go to your manager and say something along the lines of "Do you have a minute? I want to share with you this good thing that just happened." People who are good at managing up know to acknowledge the boss's role (sincerely, not sycophantically): "And I also want to thank you for giving me this chance."

Be sure, too, to give credit to any colleagues who helped, which is not only fair but underscores that you're a collaborative team player. When crafting your message, bear in mind that this is a pitch of sorts. Keep it simple, and point out the benefits to your manager. If you can do so briefly, don't be afraid to tell the story of how you pulled the success off. Remember, narrative is extremely compelling in business situations so long as there's a point to it.

As an employer, I can tell you that when this kind of pitch is done well, I don't view the person as pushy. I view her as both enthusiastic and collaborative. Unlike a self-promoter who says, "Look what I did," she's saying, "Look what we did, together."

When you're swimming with sharks

If you're lucky, you've never worked with anyone who's either unconsciously incompetent or actively seeking to stomp on colleagues as he ascends the ladder. But if you have, you're aware that even one person like this can wreak havoc in the workplace. Occasionally when I first start working with a new client, I'll be made aware that there's someone in the office who's distrusted by co-workers because he's viewed as either incompetent or vindictive—and it will be equally clear that management is blissfully unaware there's a problem. His colleagues haven't said anything, not wanting to be perceived as tattletales.

Short term, remaining silent means resigning yourself to some degree of stress and unhappiness at work. Long term, there may be consequences for your career. For example, Venture was once hired to work for a company where the recently departed head of marketing was viewed as a bungler by virtually everyone in the department. Yet no one had ever even tried to talk to senior management about the problems in the department—and now that the perceived bungler was gone, those left behind were held accountable for her mistakes.

And rightly so, to some extent. If a co-worker or manager is having a serious negative impact on team performance, and all attempts to reverse the situation by approaching the person directly have failed, someone needs to speak up and make management aware there's an issue. The response will depend largely on the way the matter is broached and how the conversation is conducted. Temperate language, concrete examples, and a straightforward, unapologetic approach can be highly persuasive. Anger, drama, innuendo, and personal attacks are almost guaranteed to backfire.

If there's a consensus that a certain individual is harming the group's performance, one approach is to choose the most diplomatic colleague to go speak to management (going en masse can create the impression of a lynch mob rather than a group of concerned corporate citizens, and in any event it becomes harder to control tone and message if a cast of thousands is in the room). The message is "I've been asked by my co-workers to speak to you about _____, because we're concerned about the impact he's having on the company." Stress the collective good, not how this individual has harmed or annoyed you personally. Avoid sweeping generalizations that include the words "never" or "always," and keep the message concise. And don't expect or demand instant results. Your goal is to sound the alarm so that higher-ups know there's a problem that's affecting productivity and morale. They need time to figure out how to respond.

On occasion, I have received emails from employees complaining about a colleague, and while I appreciate that it can be difficult to have these kinds of conversations face to face, I think it's more dangerous to conduct them electronically. Even the most carefully worded email can read like a poison pen letter when the purpose is to draw attention to someone's failings. The best and most persuasive way to raise legitimate concerns is in person, where a harsh message can be softened by body language and a calm, measured tone of voice.

Before you give up, try to change your attitude— and the corporate culture

Sometimes, after you get the job or the appointment or the account, it turns out not to be what you thought it was. The project is impossible. The new client is indecisive. The new job requires endless administrivia. The environment in the office is miserable. Depending on the situation and how hard you campaigned to get into it, you may feel your only choice is to stick it out until a reasonable period has elapsed and you can exit gracefully.

There is another option, though, when the issue involves a negative corporate culture. You can take responsibility for changing your attitude and trying to improve the culture. Just as one or two bad apples can spoil the whole bunch, one or two good ones can have an enormous positive influence on morale and the work climate. And change can start at any level. If you're working late and decide to buy coffee for everyone, instead of grousing about how unfair the hours are, that creates positive feeling. Small acts of kindness can be big game changers. And everyone is capable of a small act of kindness.

I believe it's an individual responsibility to help contribute to improving your work environment—and if you can't, to leave and find a job elsewhere. Staying in a situation you hate and complaining about everything that's wrong, but never trying to fix it, doesn't make you a martyr. It makes you complicit.

It takes courage to try to change corporate culture, particularly if you're surrounded by others who also hate it. It's scary to be the one person trying to support and improve what everyone else despises. But it is also possible, though it can't be done overnight. The way to start is by thinking of corporate culture not as something handed down to you by management but as something you and all your co-workers have a hand in creating, together. From the receptionist to senior management, change happens when people start viewing themselves as contributors and asking, Can I be more positive? Can I say things differently? Today, can I help someone I normally wouldn't help? Is there someone in a support role whose contribution is always ignored? Is there someone in a senior role who's been really helpful to me, who could now use my help?

Little things and small gestures are important—even if not to the culture, then to you personally, because you're going to feel better about yourself and your job. That's true even if the only thing you change is your own attitude: "I'm going to stop complaining and start trying to make this a better place to spend my days. So what if no one says thank you?" If you're doing it because you want thanks, that's not the right reason anyway. A positive work culture is created not because you're trying to get thanks but because you're trying to build a better place for yourself, too. It benefits you as much as it does everyone else.

The recipe for change is often pretty simple: introduce more civility, kindness, and thoughtfulness. Mix in more cheerfulness. Don't stop stirring simply because you get a negative response or the office grump is still grumpy after you tried to be nice.

However, if you try and it really is hopeless, you have to go; ultimately, working in a negative environment does harm you. That's a question to ask yourself: Is this environment helping me or harming me as an individual? Is it just a paycheque or somewhere I really want to go every day? If the former, then I hope you are brave enough to quit.

Of course, I understand that some people simply don't have any other employment options at the moment. They need the money, or lack the skills to find anything better. I do understand that coal miners aren't headed down the shaft every morning singing "Kumbaya." But if you really can't persuade anyone else to give you another job, then you need to persuade yourself to change the way you think about the one you have.

KNOWING WHEN TO SPEAK UP—OR GET OUT

Sometimes, people convince themselves that an existing corporate culture—even a corrupt or unethical one—simply can't be changed, and it's easier to just go with the flow than to make waves. Moral compromise is a temptation we all face at some point or another in our careers. Whether the temptation involves filching office supplies or robbing shareholders, everyone eventually gets an opportunity—and likely more than one—to find out what they're made of. Several times in my career, I've had to be willing to put my business in danger in order to save the things that are of intrinsic value to me as an individual. In every case, the decision hinged on whether I was willing to sacrifice my ethics in order to get or retain work.

Here's what I've learned. If you're not willing to defend your core values, you can't persuade others that you're trustworthy. Speaking up is the price of authenticity. You owe it to yourself, and to your reputation, to defend your beliefs. Yes, it will be uncomfortable and, yes, it may make you unpopular in some quarters. But trust me, so long as you're not getting on your high horse to defend the principle of not taking someone's pop from the fridge or something equally minor, you will at some point be happy you spoke up.

When you're being asked to deliver from the grey zone

A major multinational brand we were thrilled to work for once hired Venture for a relatively minor project we very much hoped would turn into something bigger. Then one day, a senior executive on the client side came to me and said, "Look, you're an approved vendor. I want you to overbill us and then cut me a cheque for the difference. I'm not doing anything wrong, I'm just going to use the money to buy tickets to hockey games for client entertainment, but our organization is so bureaucratic it would take months to get this approved. I just don't want the hassle." It was a no-brainer. I said, "If there's nothing wrong with it, why won't your company let you do it?" And that was the end of our relationship with that impressive brand.

I've never regretted that decision. It was clear-cut: I was being asked to commit fraud. Yes, the account was potentially huge, but not as huge as the downside. Along with my self-respect, I could've lost my entire business if I'd gone along with this scheme. But sometimes, the right answer isn't as clear, and you're deep into the problem before you even recognize that you have one.

If authenticity is about knowing yourself, honesty is about publicly demonstrating and defending your beliefs and principles—and it's especially important to do this when it feels uncomfortable and when you have skin in the game. You have to be willing to speak up if you disagree or if you know something is wrong—what's at stake is not just what you stand to lose in this particular circumstance but your reputation. If your actions aren't aligned with your values and beliefs, the damage to your reputation could be far more devastating than any immediate loss you might suffer.

The problem with turning a blind eye

Have you ever sat quietly and just let it pass when your boss framed an argument in a way you knew was misleading? Have you ever noticed a colleague's misconduct but said nothing because you didn't want to look like a snitch? Or even noticed a friend explaining a plan but strategically skipping over a major detail? Probably all of us have done something like this at one time or another, thinking it's no big deal.

But the consequences of turning a blind eye can be far-reaching and extremely damaging. For example, in many scandals involving senior executives billing back expenses for, say, lavish hotel stays and dry cleaning, it turns out that many people were aware of or signed off on the fraud. Often someone will surface who says, "Well, I *did* wonder about it at the time, but everyone else seemed fine with it so I didn't say anything." But in a scandal, people who had niggling doubts but didn't voice them will be shown the door along with everyone else, often with irreparably damaged reputations.

Speaking up when you believe something is wrong may have immediate consequences that feel punitive. But in the long run, if you betray your ethics and beliefs, there's no way to view that as a win.

Venture once had a client whose business represented a very large proportion of our revenue, and they knew it. They treated me and the team like they owned us. Everyone who worked on that account felt abused and unappreciated, and we were pouring in time and energy far beyond what we were being compensated to provide. Worse, they were asking us to do things that were on the grey edge of what I considered to be right, and I was starting to wonder if some of their plans might wind up having a negative impact on the company's stakeholders. I remember watching our team wilt and thinking, "I guess this is just what you have to do to keep big business."

Then I attended a meeting where I felt key facts and numbers were being misrepresented to the board before a favourable crucial vote. The issue wasn't that this would have a somewhat negative impact on Venture: to me, it was wrong. In spite of the importance of the account, I knew it was a defining moment for me. I had to draw a line for what I knew was right. So after the presentation I made myself stand up. My heart was pounding and I wasn't 100 percent sure what was about to come out of my mouth. I heard myself ask the board members, "If I told you I believe that I could prove that information to be incorrect, that the numbers have been framed in a misleading way that could damage stakeholders, would your vote be any different?"

And then I said something I definitely had not been planning to say: "If you decide to move ahead, I'm sorry, but I can't continue to work for you. Please accept my resignation, effective immediately." It was a huge business decision, one of the biggest of my life, and as soon as I walked out of the room I thought, "What have you done?" I felt sick. I had visions of having to lay off half my staff. But when I got back to the office and announced the decision, people cheered.

Ultimately, taking a stand bought me more loyalty and trust than I could ever have had if I'd hung on to the client. And taking the risk gave me credibility, so I was able to persuade the team to work even harder to help me replace the revenue. And we did, together.

In retrospect, I should've cut bait much earlier than I did. Taking a stand sooner would have been better for my staff and for me. The lesson I learned is that you have to be willing to speak up right away when something doesn't square with your values, and you have to believe that you will recover if the result of speaking up is that you lose business, or allies, or even friends. You need to persuade yourself that you will get other work, and next time, no one will ask you to compromise your beliefs to support their agenda.

Another lesson: Some people think anyone with a heartbeat is worth having as a client. Not me. If client A has a million dollars to spend and wants to partner with us and develop a shared strategy, and client B will pay two million but is abusive—I'll always choose client A. This is, by the way, why I'll never be a billionaire. To be a billionaire, I think you probably just may have to view all dollars as being created equal.

If you have to exit, do so gracefully

I used to sit on a board that at one point had to make a crucial decision about a conflict in the organization. I disagreed with the way the board wanted to handle the situation and said so. The others decided to proceed in a way that I just wasn't comfortable with, so I resigned. Soon afterward, another board member—someone who hadn't taken a stand in any way on this issue—approached me and said, "You know, it's easier to fight the good fight inside the tent than outside the tent." I don't agree with that, not if being inside a tent means throwing in my lot with a den of thieves. I never want to fight that fight that way because there's no win. I'd rather set up my own tent.

However, I didn't need to express all this on my way out of the organization. It was enough to say I disagreed and felt I needed to resign. There's no point leaving scorched earth and a trail of bodies behind you when you leave. Much better to explain your reasons calmly and exit as gracefully as you can. While standing up and delivering a tirade might give you some moral satisfaction, you'll almost certainly undo all the good you did prior to that moment.

THE COST OF PERSUASION

After your pitch succeeds, you enter into an ongoing relationship with a new partner, new employer, new client, or new investor. Or you change an existing relationship because you're being promoted or transferred or paid more money. Whatever the case, there will be fresh challenges and complications. So before you set out to persuade someone, you need to be certain that you actually want what you're asking for. Because you just might get it.

When you're focused solely on winning, you can lose sight of the big picture: if you do win, you will need to deliver, you will need to work productively with these people, and you will need to be able to handle conflicts and disagreements, which are almost inevitable. If that prospect gives you pause, take your hesitation and reluctance very seriously.

At the end of the day, when you persuade others, you're not accountable to just them. You are also accountable to yourself, which means taking responsibility for your sense of fulfillment and achievement, not just in business but in life.

Conclusion

My very first clear childhood memory is from my family's journey to Canada. (I recently checked with my mother, who confirmed this really did happen and that it's not one of those "memories" you invent as an adult.) We'd stopped over in London, England, and I was standing at the window of our hotel room in a six-storey building—a skyscraper to me—when my dad asked, "What are you looking at?" I said something like, "Nothing, I'm excited about taking the plane to Canada!" He turned me around, got down on his knee—my dad was such a teacher—and said, "When you turn back to the window, I want you to look at London. Really *look*. You're missing where you are because you're thinking about where you're going."

My dad's message—pay attention to and enjoy the journey, don't just focus on the destination—has stuck with me always. He wasn't a New Age kind of guy by any means, but he taught me the importance of relishing the moment while maintaining a sense of excitement about what's to come. Early on in my business career, I persuaded myself that I might as well enjoy the journey because who knew where I would wind up.

A lot of gurus will tell you that you need to have a fairly detailed plan and a destination in mind if you want to succeed in business. Well, as you know by now, I had neither. Sometimes I think that makes me an idiot. But most of the time I think it's a good thing because, as a result, I've always been open to opportunity. When I get up in the morning I think, "What will the day hold?" I don't spend a lot of time anticipating or worrying; I just allow the day to unfold and try to make sure I enjoy it. Now, that doesn't mean I don't have a to-do list. I do, and some days it's a mile long. But every day, I try to be very open to what might happen once I've mentally ticked off the items on my list.

I also have goals, but they're almost all qualitative: More face time with Venture employees. More new experiences. More time with my grandchildren. This isn't just because I've made money and can now afford to think about other things. My goals have always been qualitative: Be a good mom. Lead an interesting life. Learn every day. And every day I have to remind myself of these goals so they don't get lost.

Why don't I have a life plan that spells out where I hope to be a year or five years from now? Because I've learned it's highly likely that unpredictable things will happen to change even the best-laid plans. No plan could possibly account for the randomness of life itself or the curve balls it throws at us. Maybe you'll wind up falling in love with and marrying someone who lives clear across the country, where there are almost no opportunities in your field. Maybe a relative will fall ill, and you'll have to put your career on the back burner to lend a hand. Maybe there'll be an unplanned pregnancy—and congratulations, it's twins! Most big opportunities, too, are unlooked for and unexpected. I certainly never dreamed of being on a reality TV show, for example, or writing a book. And I'm pretty sure I wouldn't have been willing to assume the risk of failure that comes with every new opportunity if I'd stubbornly insisted on sticking to some predetermined plan. I wouldn't have wanted to be blown off course. All of which explains why I think that how you deal with unexpected events, how you let them influence your life and your career, is key. You need to persuade yourself that you have what it takes to deal with whatever life throws at you—and that you will jump at opportunities, even when it feels frightening.

My own plan, such as it is, consists primarily of looking for potential and opportunity in whatever path I'm on. Sometimes it's hard to find, and all I can see at first are problems. But even those are part of the adventure and can wind up changing your life in positive ways. Really tough experiences aren't fun, but weathering them can build your character and give you the confidence to take risks and seize opportunities in the future.

The future. You just don't know what it will hold, or where a talent for persuasion can help you go. Frankly, if someone had told me 10 years ago that I'd find myself where I am today, I would have said it was improbable. But I'd never have said it was impossible. I just don't think in those terms anymore.

Nor should you. Everyone—*everyone*—has potential and is capable of realizing it. Becoming a good persuader is a great start. That's a skill that can take you far. But the first obstacle to overcome is generally the most daunting: your view of your current circumstances and prospects. You have to persuade yourself of the potential on your path or you will never rise above your problems.

This is one of those commercials, as my dad called them, that most of us need to keep replaying, over and over, to persuade ourselves we can move forward. Sometimes the issue is a business problem. And other times it's personal. For instance, a few years ago, when I turned 51, I had an unpleasant encounter with a scale. I was overweight and, worse, unfit. Of course, I'd known this, but my response had been to focus on the problems involved in doing something about it—I had no time to work out, I was too tired, I was too heavy already, what was the point? When I saw the number on the scale, however, something in me snapped: self-doubt. I immediately hired a trainer, which is a luxury I feel extremely lucky to be able to afford, and she forced me to run. I knew I had to exercise, but . . . running? Was she crazy? Or just cruel? At first, I could manage only a couple of minutes at a time. But a year later, I was running a half-marathon. Once again, I'd focused on my problems so intently that I hadn't been able to see my potential.

It's never too late to change your life. But the hardest person to sell on the idea of your potential is almost always yourself. Which is why all persuasion starts with you. Before you can persuade someone else to do anything, you need to persuade yourself of your potential.

That's what I did and that's what I keep doing. And if I can do it, trust me, you can, too.

Acknowledgements

This book would not exist if Iris Tupholme at HarperCollins hadn't believed I could write it, and if my highly persuasive editor, Kate Cassaday, hadn't suggested the topic, then gracefully pried the manuscript out of my hands and worked her magic on it. Throughout it all, my agent, Rick Broadhead, went above and way beyond the call of duty to represent me as who I really am.

Kate Fillion's dedication to my story and invaluable support and efforts have made the book a true collaboration of minds. Kate, you have my trust, admiration and faith.

I also owe thanks to my fellow dragons in the den, to every entrepreneur who has come on our show, and to the incredible, multi-talented team at CBC—it's been a life-changing opportunity, and you've all taught me so much about the process of persuasion.

My most important training ground, however, has been Venture Communications. My sister-in-law Carolyn Anderson helped me get back on my feet and into the job market, an act of kindness I've never forgotten. I then had the good fortune to work with Tom Wood and Terry Lauder, my partners at Venture, who believed in me and brought me into the company more than 20 years ago. Today, I'm extremely lucky to have the support of the entire team at Venture. Without all of you I couldn't have branched out to try other endeavors, and I'm grateful every day for your creativity and hard work, as well as for the way you make me look good while keeping me humble. Jennifer Cioffi, Venture's president and my strongest ally, not only continued to take care of business while I was writing but somehow also found time to read the manuscript carefully and give me perceptive comments and incisive suggestions. Of course, the clients who have placed their trust in Venture over the many years are the reason we want to deliver great work; I can't thank each of you enough for the faith, confidence and respect you give to us and our company. As for Maria-Liisa Barnby, my executive assistant, chief supporter, and the person who makes my life possible—I don't know what I'd do without you, ML.

In my personal life, I'm blessed to be surrounded by people who cheer me on without ever sparing me the truth. My mother and my sisters helped me find my place in the world; my wonderful father, the teacher, taught me so much about life and how to enjoy it while owning my own decisions. Margot, the best friend I could ever have, has helped me weather the lows and revel in the highs. David Downer is always there for me with his love and support, as is Charlie, who makes me smile.

Finally, but firstly, I am endlessly grateful to my children; Garrett, Michael, Carley and Marayna; and my beautiful grandchildren, Carter, Colton and Hailey—all of you bring joy, meaning and true purpose to my life. You are beyond everything to me. I love you past what any words can ever hope to express.